Off Grid Living & Solar Power Simplified

2-IN-1 COMPILATION | STEP-BY-STEP GUIDE TO BECOME COMPLETELY SELF-SUFFICIENT AND DESIGN & INSTALL YOUR SOLAR POWER SYSTEM IN AS LITTLE AS 30 DAYS

Small Footprint Press

THIS COLLECTION INCLUDES THE FOLLOWING BOOKS:

OFF GRID LIVING

OFF GRID SOLAR POWER

CONTENTS

OFF GRID LIVING

INTRODUCTION

Over the past few years, there has been a sudden and powerful interest in leaving the city and finding an independent life in the country. You have probably experienced some of the same thoughts and feelings. There's been a massive departure from some of the densest population centers in the United States. There have been net population losses in New York, Nairobi, and Paris.

People are sick of the noise, the pollution, and the chaos that exists in cities. They want to live in places that feature natural beauty.

In Russia, people are leaving for country estates called *dachas*. In the UK, people are leaving London and Edinburgh for the Scottish highlands. In the USA, people are abandoning San Francisco and New York. We are seeing a great migration from cities worldwide. After the COVID pandemic started in 2019, people didn't want to feel confined anymore. They want to be able to walk outside freely. They don't want to feel dependent on strangers. They don't want to live every day feeling like they need permission.

Unsurprisingly, many people have recently been attracted to living off-grid. Living off-grid offers relief for many who have been suffocating from these feelings and are ready to get out.

Cities are strange environments that we've created for ourselves. We could have made any kind of place to live, and for some reason, we chose to stack ourselves into tiny little 40-story apartments. We decided that this was worth paying $1,800 in rent every month.

New York had the good sense to set some land aside to feature nature - Central Park. City planners had the foresight to know that if people become too separated from nature, it would crush their spirits and make them feel crazy.

Now we are at a time where we don't even remember why we wanted to live like that. Lots of people are seeing it for the first time.

But off-grid living, unfortunately, is not for everyone. While living off-grid is a wonderful lifestyle, it's a huge step to take, especially for those who don't have any experience living self-sufficiently. It takes time, effort, and money to make these changes, such as buying land far outside the city, setting up off-grid systems, and raising livestock. Furthermore, many people are held back by their assumptions about living off-grid.

There's so much to learn about this lifestyle. Throughout this book, you'll discover that some expectations are far from reality and that the things that you think are holding you back or preventing you from being able to live off-grid don't exist at all. You will learn precisely what off-grid living entails and what you need to do. Once you have all of the information needed, you will be able to make an informed decision about whether off-grid living is for you or not.

SOMETHING BETTER

Think of this book as a shopping catalog. You're building a new life, and you need to figure out all the pieces and how you will put it all together.

This book will cover many topics, but it can't teach you everything you need to know. This one book can't train you to be a plumber, electrician, outdoorsman, carpenter, and farmer. What this book can and will give you a broad understanding of living off-grid, giving you the information and options to help you decide what's best for you and your family.

Some people enjoy living a simple, minimalistic lifestyle free of modern conveniences. Other people can live a completely normal modern lifestyle off the grid. If you want to live a super minimalist, 18th-century lifestyle, that's fine. If you want a modern lifestyle off-grid, that's okay, too. It's just a matter of what you are looking for.

One topic that many people might be interested in that we won't get into is prices. Prices are constantly changing. Wind power and solar technology are improving and becoming more popular, so the prices are decreasing as it becomes more popular in the consumer market. Battery technology is getting better. There are also changes in the price of inflation and some recent political considerations that will affect the availability of imports.

For that reason, this book will not mention the cost. By the time you read this, it may be completely different. You will want to do your own shopping and figure out those costs on your own. While some things are cheaper, and there's no reason to pay more for them, you get exactly what you pay for. Suggesting you get the most expensive Gucci may not be appropriate, and also saying you should get the cheapest one available might be a terrible idea.

CHAPTER 1: IS OFF-GRID LIVING THE RIGHT CHOICE FOR YOU?

Chapter one provides an in-depth overview of what it truly means to live off-grid, what it takes to get there, and whether it's the right path for you to take.

More and more people worldwide are beginning to realize that a life away from modern societies ever-present sounds more plausible and amazing than ever. Because of recent events and the instability of modern life in general, many want to escape to their own slice of heaven, away from civilization and the traps of society.

While people in the city depend on its various systems to survive, they still need to take care of their necessities. The city lacks a sense of community where people are able to depend on each other for their daily lifestyles. Much like a lone wolf, people in the city take care of only themselves and no one else. However, they are also dependent on government structures and institutions to maintain their lifestyles.

On the opposite end, there are self-sustaining communities, where individuals function as a collective by helping each other with their various skills. Their differing skills allow them to live sustainably and sufficiently, without needing sources outside of their community!

While they depend on each other to survive, it is much different from people in the city who depend on institutions and government structures. Self-sustaining communities depend on each other to have more freedom, while people in the city depend on their systems only to be restricted by the very systems they rely on.

They live off-grid, sustaining themselves by growing their own food, raising livestock, harvesting water, and so much more. Each person in the community serves a purpose, and so they build each other up, allowing their sustainable way of living to be possible.

While you don't have to be a part of a similar community to live off-grid, they can be viewed as role models because having the mindset that you need to be alone to survive can be disadvantageous in many ways.

WHAT IS OFF-GRID LIVING?

Some people have very rigid ideas of what off-grid really entails, but in reality, off-grid living simply describes a particular lifestyle. Living off-grid is all about self-reliance and self-determination. You have to be aware of nature and what it provides.

Living off-grid isn't always easy, and it isn't for everyone, especially when just starting out. There are many things to learn and trials that will challenge you along the way. Living on your own, developing your self-reliance, and learning to take control of your own needs is not the easiest way to live a life, but it is rewarding. It's one thing to work a job that pays you good money and makes enough for a down payment on a home to live in and raise a family. There's another experience entirely of living in a home that you built.

Living off-grid usually implies being disconnected from the electrical grid, gas, municipal water supply, sewage, and telephone lines. It doesn't mean living without the things that those services provide. It means providing them for yourself.

- Living off-grid does NOT mean:
- Living in a medieval hut.
- Abstaining from modern conveniences.
- Cutting off contact from the outside world.
- Growing a beard and living in a bunker, while writing a weird manifesto.

There are many reasons why a person would choose to live off the grid. It is a lifestyle that attracts all kinds of people from all kinds of backgrounds. Ask yourself if any of these apply to you.

Green

Disconnecting from the grid means disconnecting from the energy system. Being able to produce your own energy from the sun, wind, or water is a way to reduce your environmental impact. Perhaps you just want to separate yourself from the pollution in the city.

Many people living off-grid have objections to factory farming practices and would rather grow their own food than participate in the industrial food system. You may feel better knowing exactly where your food came from. You can grow what you like and know it is free of GMOs and pesticides.

You may be well aware of the electricity you use at home. But there's also the electricity you don't see on your monthly power bill. That electricity is factored into the price of every manufactured thing you own. Some of those items are manufactured abroad in places with few environmental laws. Many of the things you own may have been built or manufactured using coal or oil energy, which are well-known pollutants. If you reduce your consumption by using the land, you can also reduce your dependence on things you disagree with.

A self-sufficient lifestyle might help you be more conscientious about your own footprint and impact on global climate change. Many people have gotten into off-grid living as part of a movement to take responsibility for their own environmental impacts. You may not be able to change the world, but you can change yourself. If enough people do that, we're all better off.

Self-Reliance

A lot of people simply like to be self-reliant. In the event of a natural disaster, self-sufficiency will not be a problem for a person living off-grid. If the power goes out, they have power. If the water becomes a problem, they have water. If the cost of food spikes or there are shortages, that will not be a problem for a family who grows their own food.

Overall, people just feel a sense of pride and accomplishment. Some people don't want to feel like they are a burden on others and that no one else burdens them. You gain a certain sense of security when you know that you don't need to rely on others. If you only need to rely on yourself and you are reliable, then you'll never be disappointed.

If you want to strike it out, make it on your own, and build something that you can be proud of, homesteading might be the thing for you.

Privacy

We all like our privacy: We like quiet and solitude. If you are inclined to walk around your house in the nude, you can do so without worrying about any neighbors peeking into the windows. In fact, you could probably just walk outside completely nude without any fear of phone calls to the police.

If you want to have guests over, play music, and have a bonfire and a good time outside, no one will live close enough to you to complain about it. No one is going to come and knock on your door and tell you to keep down the noise.

Likewise, you don't have to deal with anybody else's noise. When you live in the city, you become accustomed to a lot of ambient noise. You have to hear traffic and cars honking their horns. The occasional car alarm goes off for no apparent reason at 1:00 a.m.; babies scream so loud that you can hear them through the walls of your apartment; and dogs bark, bravely protecting a homeowner from the dangerous pizza delivery guy who just arrived.

Being isolated can also separate you from the problems in the city. If you live in a place with a lot of crime and violence, it tends to stay in that area and not spread too far. Having a place relatively isolated is less likely to be targeted, so long as you take the right precautions.

Investment

You don't have to be a hippie or a bearded mountain man to live off-grid. Sometimes, it just makes sense financially. A large off-grid project can have a significant upfront cost, but over time, it can easily pay for itself from the savings on electric, water, gas, and food bills. Living off-grid may simply make sense for people trying to be thrifty.

If you buy or build a home in a very remote location, it may be way too expensive to get utilities out to your location. For practical reasons, connecting to the grid might just be unrealistic for you—this is more common than you think. Those who have their homes built very high in the mountains or deep into the woods or countryside, without many neighbors, might decide that off-grid living is considerably less expensive than paying to have pipes and electrical lines built all the way to the grid to hook it up.

People who invest in homes often build off-grid homes to rent out to vacationers. Most people don't want to live in a remote place, but many people would love to vacation in a place like that. Making a remote and rustic off-grid location as a rental or vacation destination through one of the online hotel alternative websites could be a very remunerative enterprise.

Developing an off-grid home can require a good chunk of change. However, all of that money is an investment. Every addition you develop adds to the value of the land and will come back to you when you sell—provided there is no terrible disaster, knock on wood.

There's been an increased interest in leaving the cities in the last few years and people are escaping into rural areas. One can probably expect that the land's value will increase over time rather than decrease. For that reason, having a self-sufficient and isolated spot that appeals to people trying to escape city life could be a valuable property to flip.

HOW DO I KNOW IF OFF-GRID LIVING IS FOR ME?

Frankly, it might not be. Off-grid living is not for everybody. It takes a certain kind of personality to take on such a project and commit to it. It takes a lot of self-reliance and eagerness to learn.

People have become very accustomed to convenience. Convenience is another word for time—as in saving time. Anything convenient saves time, but there is also a cost. Fast food is convenient. Ordering cheap things online is convenient. Sometimes, there are things more valuable than convenience. Also, the time that we are trying to save is just being wasted on other frivolous things.

These are some qualities that might determine if you are the kind of person who can do it. You don't need all of them; one is enough, but the more, the better.

Self-Starter

If you like projects, this is a great way to live. You will never run out of things to do. Many people make their home their primary hobby. Are you the kind of person who thinks about a good way to fix a squeaky garage door? Or the kind of person who builds a shed? If you're the kind of person who loves keeping busy and working with their hands, you are in luck.

There are always new ideas you have for additions and upgrades. Once your home is all put together, you'll start imagining other things you could build, such as a sauna or a guest house. Once you are done with those, you may consider what it would take to build an artificial pond. If this sounds like you, keep reading.

Autodidact

That's not a type of dinosaur: An autodidact is a person who teaches themselves rather than being taught by others. You will need to learn a lot to live off-grid. If you don't like learning, this lifestyle will not work for you as learning will always be important.

Starting this life will make you a jack of all trades very quickly. To achieve absolute self-sufficiency, you will have to learn plumbing, electrical, farming, animal care, local law, and many other skills. Some people see that and want nothing to do with that. Others see a list like that and get excited.

If you like learning and are an inquisitive person who enjoys figuring things out and discovering new things, you will have plenty of opportunities. You will discover all the things you didn't know that you needed to know, and there are a lot.

Able to Follow Through on Commitments

You were meant to be someone who isn't a quitter. Depending on how you develop your land, there can be a significant initial investment. It's possible to get started with $10,000, but depending on various factors, it could cost more. If you aren't serious about it, you could easily waste a lot of time and money.

Pioneers and homesteaders of previous centuries did it with a lot less than we have available. Lucky for you, more tools and technologies are available to you than they had.

By definition, you won't have an infrastructure around you that has been built up over a century by thousands of governments and financial corporations. You have to develop your own infrastructure from the bottom up. Over the long term, it can pay for itself.

This isn't like a month-long free trial at a gym or using a subscription service for a phone app. It's not the kind of thing you can half do half-heartedly. If you are a person who likes to finish what they start, and someone who doesn't rush into things, you have the right personality to live off-grid.

A Love for Nature

Last but not least, if you are looking to live off-grid somewhere that is far away from other people, you should be a person who genuinely loves nature. You are going to be surrounded by a lot of it.

Living off-grid means living in tandem with nature. You have to cooperate with it. Mother Nature decides when it rains, when the sun shines, and when the wind blows. While not everyone feels comfortable feeling at the mercy of nature, other people don't feel like they are at nature's mercy, but rather they are adapting to what nature prescribes. It's a very different attitude.

Maybe you like living in a city where it's easy to find things you need within a five-minute drive, and you don't like the unpredictability of nature. If you like gardening and animals, you'll have plenty of time with them. If you are someone who loves hiking, skiing, fishing, hunting, and exploring, then this is where you want to be. Are you someone who loves campfires and loves to have their morning coffee on a porch overlooking a beautiful landscape? If so, you have come to the right place.

Healthy and Fit

People with medical issues requiring regular treatments and needing to be close to the hospital or visit a clinic regularly are at greater risk if they live far away. Being off-grid doesn't mean you can't be close to a hospital, but if you need a hospital to be close, be sure to factor that in. If you plan on doing the work yourself, you should be healthy and able. People who use wheelchairs might have a very rough time with it. However, if you're in a wheelchair and can build your dream home, that would be very impressive and inspiring.

If you aren't strong or have good cardio, that problem will solve itself. You'll be chopping and carrying wood, building fences, and other physical activities, plus a cellar without junk food—that will get you in a fitter state in no time.

START SMALL

Living off the grid also doesn't have to be 100% complete on day one. Sometimes, the smartest way to start is to start small. Once you have a good piece of land with all the features you need, you can get a trailer for relatively cheap to park there. That's a good place to start.

You can buy any water you need and bring it to your location. If you're ready now, go and do it. Take it one step at a time. For most water systems, you'll need a pump. That means you'll need power. Power comes first.

You can start with a gas-powered generator until you can create something more permanent. It won't be long before you've set up a sustainable power system, such as using solar power. Once that's up, you won't need a generator, then you'll be off the electrical grid.

When you get a good or more-developed method of getting clean water, you can stop buying it. You may have just put out some rain barrels to start with, and that's fine. That'll help supplement any water that you are purchasing. Then, you'll be off the water grid.

You can rely on the grocery store when you begin and slowly phase that out as you build your garden and greenhouse and build a coop to raise some chickens. Then you'll be self-sufficient for food.

There's no reason to start with the expectation that you will be completely self-sufficient on day one. Frankly, that's very unrealistic unless you can afford to have people come and completely design your project from the ground up before you even move in. Start small and build out. Develop what you need to as you go.

As we say later on in this book multiple times, there is so much to learn. The best way to learn new things is to do them, so don't overwhelm yourself with many projects. Find one goal that you can accomplish and work on that. When it's done, continue to the next thing. If you come across any problems along the way, you'll figure them out and learn how to fix them. By the time you've moved to your next project, you'll already be an expert in whatever you just resolved.

You can live off-grid within 30 days, but you cannot build a gigantic off-grid compound with every luxury in 30 days. We don't know if it's possible to lay the foundation, build a house, and install plumbing and wiring in 30 days. In some places, we don't think it's even possible to get a permit for construction within 30 days.

However, you can begin the moment that you have land. If you start small, you can be out there next month building toward something, so if you want to do it, sincerely, do it.

MINDSET AND ATTITUDE

The off-grid mentality requires a balanced view of optimism and pessimism. You will need optimism to do the work and to believe in yourself that it can be done. It also needs pessimism because you will need to understand that things will go wrong—things that you cannot predict and things that you should be able to anticipate. Your mantra should match that of the Scouts of America: Always be prepared. Just because your electricity is working doesn't mean that something won't happen to stop the electricity. Just because you have a car and can leave doesn't mean that car will always work. Something happens to the car, and an emergency requires you to get yourself or someone else you live with to a hospital. What is plan B? If plan B fails, what is plan C?

Attitude and mindset are intangible things that you need to equip yourself with. You can't anticipate everything, so you will have to figure it out as you go along. You read this book and probably visited websites, read articles, and watched videos on the Internet, but there will always be things you don't know, like the weight of 14 ounces of mercury. There are also the things you don't know that you don't know. You can only learn these things when experience places them in front of you, and without any preparation, you will have to adapt and be creative.

One thing to keep in mind is what it means to live isolated or far away from other people. If you are from an urban or suburban area, you take a lot of things for granted. You have to understand what it means to be self-reliant in the context of living far away from people.

Remember that if something goes wrong on your property, you are the first line of defense. If something breaks down, you are the closest person to be able to fix it. You're not going to be able to rely on a landlord to come and have a look at it later the same day. If you need professional help, you'll have to call them up, and they'll have to drive out to you.

Maximize your time and get plenty of supplies when you go to town. You will want to have big trips if you're far from town. That means any shopping you want to do, you should choose a day and get everything done all at once—buying bulk and getting lots of stuff. That means also thinking well in advance about what you will need, not just what you want for dinner tonight. You can't just go downstairs to the Bodega and pick up a sandwich.

If you were injured, you might be far from a hospital. For this reason, we strongly recommend that everyone get some kind of first aid training but especially if you live far away from the nearest emergency room. Living alone, far away from other people, can be risky. If you are not healthy or if you're not doing well, then you probably should have other people with you just in case. Something like a heart attack is a problem or much less lethal if you can expect an ambulance to arrive within seven minutes. However, if the nearest ambulance is 29 minutes away, you might be in for a lot of trouble.

This also means self-defense. When you live in an isolated area, the chances that someone will come and mug you, break into your house, or rob you are lower. However, if someone does try to come to your house with intentions, the police may be very far away. For that reason, you will be your own first and last line of defense. That could be surveillance cameras or security lights that detect motion. That could mean being armed. The point is, if it's just you out there, it may mean that nobody's coming to help.

Not having stores and other people available to help you quickly means you need to do what survivalists do. Any person who's into wilderness survival will tell you that you need multiple redundancies. That means if one of your pieces of equipment fails, you need to have a backup. When you are building your system, you will want to integrate multiple redundancies throughout it. That means multiple overlapping systems. If you can get electricity from two or more sources—if one of those sources goes down—you'll always have another as a backup. If you can get water from more than one source, if you have a problem like a pump failing, then it won't be nearly as bad. This is especially true if you are relying on a car. Suppose something goes wrong with your vehicle, and you need to leave the property in a hurry. In that case, you aren't going to have a ride-sharing driver just down the block, so you want to make sure that whatever vehicle you use is in tip-top condition and don't leave anything to chance.

You have to think ahead more than you would in a city. You have to think further in the future about living without your food and about possible problems with your water and power. You have to think about your health and safety. When aid is always close, you don't have to think about these things. When there's always a grocery store a couple of miles away, you don't think about storing your food to last through the winter. A huge part of living an off-grid mindset is not preparing for the worst—not because it's likely but because something bad will happen eventually. Like the various Scouts of America say, always be prepared.

Kids

Going off-grid as a single person or spouse has certain natural advantages. You only need to care for the needs of two people. Going alone is dangerous because if something were to happen to you, no one would come looking for you. If you live with a spouse, someone will wonder why you didn't go back home.

Having children with you living off-grid has a lot of advantages and a lot of difficulties tied up with it. Children have the power to contribute more and more as they grow older, and when they're very young, they consume more than they produce. A six-year-old can help out in small ways, but they need more help than they can give. Around the time a child is ten, their contributions to the family and the consumption should be about breakeven. So, for the first decade of human life, they need more than they give. This means that adults need to produce more than they need to cover the difference.

Plus, what is crucial in raising kids is education. Depending on how off-grid you live, you might not have realistic access to schools. You might have ideological disagreements with how the schools are handled because of religious or political differences. Maybe you think that you can educate your children better than a state employee. In that case, you will have to homeschool your kids. Perhaps you are perfectly content with the education system, and you have an easy way for your children to go to school and come back. That's perfectly fine. You know what is best for your kids and family better than anyone else.

KEY CHAPTER TAKEAWAYS

- **Lesson #1: What Living Off-Grid Truly Means**

Living off-grid doesn't have to mean being disconnected from everyone and everything. You can still live a comfortable, connected life as long as you practice self-sufficiency and sustainability. Remember, you can make this lifestyle work for the kind of life you dream of.

- **Lesson #2: Off-Grid Living Can be For You**

Living off-grid requires you to have many responsibilities, so you need to be someone who likes to stay busy with tasks each day, takes the initiative to learn, loves nature, strives to be healthy and fit, and is committed to making things work. Decide whether this kind of lifestyle is the right choice for you.

- **Lesson #3: Start Small For Your Journey**

Take on your journey step-by-step, no matter how small. Plan an ideal situation for yourself and be patient as you take on new projects little by little. Not everything has to be perfect already. Things take time; your projects don't have to and shouldn't be the end-all immediately. Build slowly and carefully and do things on your own time.

- **Lesson #4: The Off Grid Mindset**

To have an off-grid mentality, you need a perfect balance of confidence and pessimism. You must always be confident in your abilities to make things work and anticipate any unfortunate situation. You must be completely prepared for anything, so anticipate possible setbacks, emergencies, and disasters and make the necessary arrangements to prepare for them.

So, What Does This All Means For You?

It's your choice to take charge of your life and make the changes. There are many things to consider, but ultimately, the decision lies in the kind of person you are, your determination, and your desires for your and your family's lives.

You probably realize that a self-sufficient life is more challenging to achieve. You'll learn in-depth information throughout this book, but if you want more hands-on learning and insider resources, you'll want to book a call with us today.

Take control of your life and transform everything you know about an off-grid lifestyle. Achieve it faster and easier than you could ever imagine.

Off Grid Mindset Check-in Exercise

Before we proceed with the rest of the book, let's first explore where you are right now in your Off Grid Journey.

Below, rate yourself on a scale of one to five on how accurate the statements are for you -- a score of one means "not accurate," and a score of five means "very accurate."

After you have rated yourself according to the statements, add the sum total of your scores, then read "What Your Score Really Means" to determine the outcome of your results.

Check-in Statement	Rating
I am completely sure that I want to live off-grid.	

I have an idea of what it takes to be self-sufficient.	
I know what my responsibilities will be when I live off-grid.	
I have an idea of a budget for my off-grid living expenses.	
I have a timeline for myself to live off-grid.	
I have begun making plans for my journey.	
I know how and what I will eat once I live off-grid.	
I am aware of the reasons I have for living off-grid.	
I know the basic fundamentals needed to live off-grid.	
My expectations and assumptions about living off-grid are in line with its realities.	
TOTAL SCORE:	

What Your Score Really Means

> **Score: 0 - 15**
>
> **The Fundamentals of the Off Grid Mindset are Still Missing**

The news here is that your current knowledge about living off-grid is missing at its core. You might be feeling a bit clueless about things, or you may even have no idea where to start. It can be a steep learning curve for those just starting out, but the good news is you can fix it.

At this stage, knowing more about the fundamentals of living off-grid is the best place to start. Understanding how it works and your responsibilities will give you a better idea of how things will go for you. Studying more about it from the chapter will help you get over the hump and eventually lead you to know where you need to be.

Score: 16 - 30

Reviewing Will Enlighten Your Mindset

Your knowledge on living off-grid is getting there, but there are some tweaks you'll need to fix. Learning won't be enough if you cannot retain the information you get. So, throughout the chapter, take note of all the responsibilities you'll be taking on as you live off-grid. Make sure to review everything you'll need to plan and prepare, such as choosing a power system or water system beforehand as an example.

Score: 31+

You're Ready to Proceed to Planning to Live Off Grid

You already have a good understanding of being self-sufficient and your responsibilities once you begin your venture. Now it's time to plan everything. Having knowledge won't help you in your journey if you don't choose to apply it as well. It's time to take action.

When you plan, it's good to set short-term and long-term goals. Ask yourself what timeline you would like to complete certain tasks. You can also begin by listing down everything you need to learn and plan for. From there, writing out your budget and your plan of action will surely help you get things in order.

CHAPTER 2: LOCATION, LOCATION, LOCATION

Chapter two will focus on how you can look for the perfect land for your future home, the best locations all over the world and in the United States to live off-grid, and the factors to consider when you finally decide on your plot of land.

Imagine this: you finally have your perfect off-grid home. You have a generous plot of arable land, a charming house you call your own, and maybe even some farm animals strutting around.

The sun has risen, and you wake up to a view of rolling hills, a bright blue sky, and soft sunlight coming in through your window. It's so serene that you can't help but smile right as you get out of bed. Your home is so pleasantly warm and cozy despite the cold weather outside. You have power to heat your home and running water to boil for your morning coffee.

You step out to collect fresh eggs from your coop, sweet honey from your colony, and creamy goat milk straight from your backyard, just in time for breakfast. You breathe in a gentle breeze drifting by, and it smells so fresh and crisp as if it had just rained.

You spend the rest of your day tending to your garden and animals, reading a lovely book, with nothing else to worry about but to take care of yourself, your home, and your loved ones.

Of course, imagining your future home is far easier than making it happen. When you start to get serious about living off-grid, you'll find many things to learn, one of which is looking for the best land and location for your future home.

This is one of the most challenging and crucial parts of your journey because once you buy that land, there's no return from it besides shelling out hard-earned cash. And none of us wants that.

That's why before you even decide, you need to set factors in place to keep you in the right direction. If you have no idea what to even consider at first and where to start looking for land, you can quickly become one of those people who buy a place out of excitement but end up realizing it's not close to how they envisioned it to be.

You see, there are several factors to remember when choosing a location. How important each factor is for you will determine your priorities and where you'll purchase land. You can't have your dream off-grid home without thorough research, and since this takes a lot of time, you might reach your goals a bit farther down the road than expected.

And that's why in this chapter, you'll get a rundown of everything you'll need to keep in mind when you start choosing your land and location. You'll also get a complete outline of the best states to live off-grid in the United States and even countries worldwide. These will automatically rule out the wrong places for you and shine a light on the right ones! You won't have to trade in those precious hours anymore for research; instead, start working on your goals.

After reading this, you'll be ready with a checklist and a design concept of your ideal off-grid home. Your own beautiful home tucked away in paradise, with total freedom and basking in nature, are within reach, all at your fingertips as you flip through these pages.

When you plan to live off-grid and look for your own location, you must remember how you should treat that area as your own sacred place. You must learn how to show respect, importance, and care for it, similar to how the Native American Indians do.

The historical values of Native American Indians hold a deep respect and appreciation for nature. Because of this, they made sure to take care of their surroundings, including the lives of humans, animals, trees, and plants.

As a community, their daily toils centered on maintaining the space around them and building up resources. Wherever they were in America, Native American Indians held a pearl of similar wisdom: that when you take care of nature, nature will take care of you. They knew that each part of the Earth was crucial for their overall survival. Each part was dependent on the other to thrive. And for nature to do its part, humans must also step in and offer care for them.

These values that the Native American Indians held so tightly are not as revered now in modern cultures. But now, it's time to look past ourselves and find a more profound outlook on how the world works. We must observe and appreciate how nature plays a huge part in caring for us, so we must do the same for it.

Living off-grid also means living off the land. The place you select will have more impact on your off-grid lifestyle than any other factor.

Living off-grid is dealing with the uncertainty of nature.

Choosing a place is a tremendous commitment. If you are going to put all the work into making a place sustainable, it needs to be the right place. You don't want to put a lot of time, money, and energy into something only to realize that it can't work for you. You need to really plan ahead. If you are close with your family, then being far apart from them might be a deal-breaker.

Location will determine a lot about the way you live. Your access to water, the soil, and other natural features will inform what energy sources and other resources are available to you. The laws can be as important, if not more important, in determining how you get your water and electricity, how you heat and cool your home, and even what you eat. Make no mistake: Choosing where you live is going to be the most crucial decision, and there are many factors you need to balance.

How to Find the Perfect off-Grid Location

What is important to you will ultimately depend on you. No one can better determine what your needs are and what kind of life you prefer. As we said in the introduction, this book is like a catalog of options that you can choose from.

Soil

If you are going to be doing any farming, the quality of the soil is going to be very important. You don't want to put all the energy into starting a farm on land that won't give anything to yield. An easy way to determine if the land is good is just to simply look around. Are other people farming in this area? If they are, there's a good chance they know what they are doing and are using farmland.

This isn't a deal-breaker by any means. If the soil isn't great, you can buy soil at any home improvement store, add your own nitrogen, and use your compost to keep the mineral-rich earth. Using your own earth, you can build a garden using raised garden beds for vegetables and herbs.

Not all locations are appropriate for certain kinds of farming. Depending on the season, soil, and climate, certain crops will be more amenable than others. For example, you aren't likely to find many tomato farmers in Alaska.

Climate

When living off-grid, you are dependent on nature to provide for you. That should go without saying, but the climate will be crucial to how you organize your life. Different climates have different advantages and disadvantages that you will need to weigh to make the life you want.

Warmer climates are usually suitable for planting. However, you will have to deal with the problem of cooling yourself and any animals you have. It's much harder to cool down than it is to warm up.

Likewise, wetter climates usually mean more water. They also mean humidity, which isn't great for humans but is excellent for plants. Humidity also usually corresponds with plant growth. Many plants can block out the wind and sun, making generating electricity more difficult if you rely on solar and wind.

A nearby pond might be great for drawing water and raising fish, but it might also be a potential breeding ground for mosquitoes.

Dry environments tend to be more comfortable. Arid areas also usually have more sun and wind, which is great for generating power. However, it may mean that getting water is more difficult or more expensive. Getting water is very important. Humans consume a lot of it, and your plants and animals will, too.

One elementary and important consideration is whether you can even reach your plot of land. Suppose your home is far away from the nearest road and you have lots of snowfall. In that case, you might be at risk of getting snowed in, and unlike other people who live in the city and subdivisions, there is no truck already on its way to plow the snow for you. Having a long road and heavy snow could mean you'll need a truck that you can mount a snow plow onto.

That's a lot of double-edged swords. There are advantages, and there are drawbacks to everything. You have to seriously consider and weigh what is right for you.

Growing Season

Tied to climate and soil is the growing season. Historically, farmers plant in the spring, grow in the summer, harvest in the fall, and rely on their surplus during the winter. If you are going to be heavily reliant on producing your own food, you will want a longer and more productive season. You probably won't be growing much during the winter.

Building a greenhouse can maximize productivity and extend the season if it is short. The more you grow and effectively store, the deeper you can fill your pantries and enjoy those supplies throughout winter. Luckily if you run out of food, you still have the option of driving to the local grocery store.

Water

The importance of water cannot be understated. When living in arid places like parts of New Mexico and Australia, people depend on water infrastructure. There is very little rainfall and very little access to natural water supplies.

Without water, you cannot drink; maintain plants or animals; take showers, cook most foods, or even wash your clothes or dishes. You need water, and getting water is your most important and challenging task.

Your primary water source will come from a well supplemented by rainfall. If you are lucky enough to have rivers or creeks that pass through your property or a pond—provided that there are no regulations against using that water—you can also use those.

The Law

This is the least fun and interesting part of off-grid living, but it is vital. Making an error about the law can cost you a lot of money and trouble down the road. There's no use using common sense because laws often don't make sense. Don't assume that you are doing it right without checking first.

The different states have completely different regulations regarding building structures, digging wells, hunting, fishing, and everything else you can imagine. The number of laws is so vast and complex that we even have an entire profession dedicated to arguing about what the laws actually are. They're called lawyers, and even they need to specialize in particular areas of the law because there are so many.

If you aren't sure whether something you were doing is legal or not, we strongly recommend that you don't just guess. You need to investigate for yourself. Reach out to any local boards or administrative offices that handle that sort of thing—that means the DNR or the mayor's office. Even if they can't help you, they may be able to point you toward someone else who can.

Another useful resource is people who are also already living the lifestyle you are working towards. They have most likely already experienced legal hiccups along the way, and if you can reach out to them, they can save you a lot of trouble. Look around on the Internet for forums and groups that are into off-grid living. If you can find others who live in a particular area, they might have answers to your questions.

Never ever buy land in a subdivision. Subdivisions are parcels that are pieces of land, part of a larger covenant agreement. If you have land that is attached to such an agreement, that means you are going to have a lot more rules that you need to follow. It's like having a homeowners' association and a bunch of neighbors who might have very strong opinions about what you can and cannot do with your land. This isn't just true in the suburbs. You can also find properties like this in rural areas, so be sure to avoid this.

Keep in mind that agriculturally zoned land tends to be cheaper than residential or commercial land. If you can, buy agricultural land and make sure it allows for livestock ownership and farming. If you buy land zoned incorrectly, you might find that many things you want to do are not legal.

Believe it or not, some counties legally require you to hook up to city water. Whether you want to or not, you may be forced to pay for installing the pipes and hook up. This can cost you up to $10,000 or more. The same goes for electricity. Some states legally require you to be on the grid. The whole point is to be off-grid, so don't go buying a place where you are not allowed to be off-grid.

There are also considerations of covenants and regulations about whether or not you can have a camper or trailer on your land, or rules about mineral rights or requirements about a permanent foundation. You might find that a big part of choosing your land is whether you can negotiate the obstacles your state and local government set up.

Taxes and Exemptions

Tax laws are quite different from state to state. You may have to pay a rather hefty fee annually, depending on the size and location of the land you are using. Depending on your budget, this cost could be an essential part of your evaluation of where to homestead. Some places have no income tax; some places have low land taxes. These are things to take into account, depending on your finances.

Certain states offer certain tax write-offs that you can avail yourself of. A few states, including Oregon and Utah, offer tax deductions for using green energy on your property. Some states also offer tax breaks for those who use their land for farming. If you are building a new sizable grow operation, you might find that these rebates are worth your while.

Some states offer what's called the homestead exemption. That means that if you happen to go bankrupt and a certain portion of your land is filed as a homestead, then that portion of your land cannot be taken by creditors. The old traditional form of pharmacy went under during bad times, and workers would ultimately lose their homes—this is a law designed to protect people like that. You may not be terribly concerned about going bankrupt, which may not be a factor for you, but it is nice to have everything the same just in case.

Cost of Living

Money always matters. You may have a lot, or you may have a little. Your budget is your business, and budgeting might be a crucial factor for you.

Typically, the farther you are from the city, the cheaper the land will be. People will pay a pretty penny to be close to a hospital or inside a good school district. The farther away you are from all of that, the less you need to spend. You might have to balance how close you want to be to civilization with how much you're willing to spend.

Banks and mortgage companies like to sell you houses, not dirt. Sometimes, finding banks willing to finance vacant land can be challenging. Often, the banks selling empty land charge more in terms of interest or down payments. One way around this is to work out a deal directly through owner financing. In this case, the bank operates as an intermediary where the lending agreement is directly between the current owner and the prospective buyer. The bank just gets a taste of mediating.

Everyone lives on different budgets; some places are more expensive than others. The prices of things are based on whatever the market will bear. Things you want, such as natural beauty, will also be valuable to other people. This is one reason locations like Geneva and Southern California are so expensive. Both have great weather. Switzerland has access to a beautiful mountain range and nature, and California has an entire coastline and beaches galore where you can search. And of course, living near people with money costs money.

If you were living in a particularly remote area, things would simply be more expensive because of the challenge of supplying areas. Areas in or around Alaska or island systems in places like Canada and Southeast Asia can be quite pricey because shipping to them is costly and complex.

Natural Disasters

God forbid that you should experience any serious natural disaster. The odds that your home will be affected by one like that is usually pretty remote, but it shouldn't be ignored. You need to investigate if the area you're homesteading in is particularly vulnerable to flooding, tornadoes, or hurricanes. You need to think about these things and have a plan ready so that you will know ahead of time and have a way to protect yourself.

Communication is essential for this. If you live in a tornado country, you definitely need access to the national weather service and a place to take shelter, such as a cellar. You want to be the last person to know there's a tornado, with no good way of getting away or taking shelter.

Homeschooling

School is very important for people who have kids or plan on having kids. It matters in terms of quality but also accessibility.

If you live far away from schools, you might not have a bus that comes by your home. It might not be realistic to drive your kids to school and back, depending on the distance. Or perhaps you want to homeschool for ideological reasons.

Whatever the case may be, homeschooling might be important to you. Not all states are equally permissive about homeschooling. You will want to look into this and ensure that your state will allow it if that's important to you.

If you do decide to take the homeschooling route, now is a better time than ever. Homeschooling has come a long way over the last 20 years. There are all kinds of programs and lessons that can be bought online. There are many ways to meet with other parents and children to help them learn to socialize.

Access to Civilization

Some people can't safely live in an isolated area. If you have an illness requiring frequent doctor visits or hospital visits, it might not be the best idea to live far from access to medical services.

Living off-grid does not mean you are living like a caveman or a 19th-century Canadian lumberjack. Being off a utility grid does not mean being off a social grid. You don't need to be socially isolated from other people. In fact, every psychologist will strongly recommend that you do not isolate yourself from other people. Just because you are living off-grid does not mean that you can't go into town to pick up supplies or go out to dinner or sports events.

The distance you are from your closest ER or grocery store might make a massive difference in driving time, gas, and emergency response. Being located in a spot that is difficult for an ambulance to get to might be a deal-breaker.

BEST STATES FOR OFF-GRID LIVING

These are ten of the best states for living off-grid. This is not a top ten list; they aren't ranked from worst to best. Each of these places has its own strengths and weaknesses. Which is "best" depends on your needs and wants. No place is perfect for everyone, but there is a place that is perfect for you.

Look over this list and measure the pros and cons; from there, you can decide which place you feel is best.

North Carolina

"Nothing could be finer than to be in Carolina in the morning." North Carolina is a fantastic farm state, and many fellow homesteaders are out there because of their very friendly laws. Plus, since it's a great farming state with a long growing season and beautiful agriculture, it also happens to be expensive. North Carolina is a lovely state, and you get what you pay for.

Pros

- It is a big farm state
- There are a lot of homesteaders, and it is ideal out west
- Green rebate
- Homestead declaration
- It has a long growing season

Cons

- Expensive land
- They are tight on homeschooling

Michigan

The wolverine state is not a bad choice at all. One of its most obvious and valuable features is that there is a ton of fresh water. Enormous lakes surround the state, and tons of smaller lakes are on the interior. No one living in Michigan is too far away from a place to take a boat out to relax or to go fishing.

Michigan already has a substantial homesteading community, and you are better off finding plenty of other like-minded people. The more north you decide to venture in the state, the more open land there is.

One thing Michigan isn't running out of is fresh water. Michigan has all four seasons, although winters may seem a little long. The land is good for raising crops, but the season might be short. Maximize the season.

Michigan is also a great state for fishing. There are more lakes, and you can count plenty of salmon and trout that you can fish.

Michigan also has a large homesteading community. Having people who are also taking on the same project is always great; by making friends with others, you can learn a lot. In recent years, the price of living in Michigan has increased, so consider that.

Pros

- The soil is good
- It has short seasons
- There is a lot of water for fishing
- There are many other homesteaders

Cons

- The laws can be strict
- It has middle-of-road taxes
- It has complicated homeschooling laws

Tennessee

The beautiful state of Tennessee is one of the most underrated in the Union. Like North Carolina, Tennessee is a state that is very friendly to homesteaders. It also happens to be the state that hosts The Great Appalachian Homesteading Conference. While Idaho is getting a lot of love right now, the people of Tennessee should be glad that they haven't been discovered quite yet.

People living off-grid are generally more likely than most others to get nailed with a panoply of natural disasters. Anyone living out there needs to take the proper precautions.

Pros

- It has a mild climate with four distinct seasons
- It's a beautiful state with great state and national parks
- The cost of living is relatively low—it's about 10% less than the national average
- There's good dirt for farming, especially in the west
- There is plentiful water
- Rural Homesteading Land Grant
- It has a homestead exemption

Cons

- There are lots of natural disasters, including earthquakes, tornadoes, and floods

Indiana

Like many other places on this list, Indiana is great for farming. They've got a good assortment of land and a good growing season; they aren't hurting for water. At present, picking up rural land in Indiana may be tricky, so be sure to keep an eye out well in advance if you have any desire to move out there. One last thing, and we say this with all due respect, Indiana, besides homesteading, is a pretty dull state. If you like boring, that's great. If that's going to be a problem for you, maybe look around for other items on this list.

Pros

- It mostly features farmland
- It has a longer growing season
- It has good homeschooling systems
- The income tax is good

Cons

- It might not be easy to get land
- It has high sales taxes

Iowa

Iowa is, of course, an excellent farming state. They offer generous tax credits for farmers and homestead exemption, which is definitely a big help.

With no disrespect to the good people of Iowa, Iowa is not a very pretty state. It is mostly rolling planes filled with corn, wheat, and soybeans. It doesn't enjoy the beautiful forests of Northern California and Iowa. It doesn't have the mountains of Tennessee and Colorado. It doesn't have beautiful bodies of water like Michigan or Florida. Iowa has many good qualities, but the natural aesthetic is not one of them.

Pros

- It is a big farming state
- It offers tax credits for farming

- There are homestead exemptions
- It has low taxes
- Homeschooling is allowed

Cons

- There are a lot of floods
- Let's be honest. Iowa isn't beautiful. Sorry, Iowa.

Virginia

Virginia is a fantastic farming state and always has been. They have plentiful rainfall, and they have access to the ocean. It's a trendy state for a good many reasons.

However, the problem with popular states is that they attract many people. Many people mean more expensive land, higher cost of living, and higher taxes. Unfortunately, there are many disadvantages of living in a city, except those disadvantages will follow you into the more isolated areas.

Pros

- There's great farming—Virginia is a farming state and always has been.
- It has good rainfall
- It has low property tax
- You can sell back electricity to power
- It is very popular

Cons

- The land is expensive
- The cost of living is high
- They are strict on homeschooling
- The state is quite disaster-prone: hurricanes and flooding

Oregon

Once you leave the Portland area, you will feel like you're in a completely different country. Oregon is a geologically beautiful state and very wet. Finding water in Oregon is as difficult as throwing a rock and waiting to hear it splash on something. You'll pay a hefty income tax if you make a lot of money, though.

Pros

- There are no sales taxes
- There's lots of water
- There are few natural disasters

- It has a green energy tax rebate
- It's very rainy

Cons

- It has a high income tax

Missouri

Missouri is very friendly to homesteads. They are very light with regulations, which is a significant hurdle to overcome in more regulated states. The state is also geologically diverse, and one part of the state will be quite different from another one. In short, it's easier to do what you want with your property.

Missouri gets a lot of rain. An average of about 40 inches per year is legal to collect rainwater in barrels ("Average Annual Precipitation for Missouri," n.d.). Summers are sweltering and can get very humid, but the winters are a little milder. By that, we mean a longer growing season but more need to keep your home cool.

Pros

- It has long seasons
- It has a good amount of rainfall
- It's a great place for homeschooling
- There are solar incentives

Cons

- The winters are rough
- It has high income taxes
- There are natural disasters like tornadoes and floods

Wyoming

The cowboy state is a strong option. It is the least populated state in the Union, and the land is cheap. There is plenty of open space for solar and wind. However, sometimes too much of a good thing is a bad thing. Wyoming can have very powerful windstorms that are so strong that your roads are shut down for the safety of drivers. If you are in a location that is vulnerable to wind, you could find yourself in some difficulty. Also, your windmills might be great in most conditions, but powerful winds can sometimes be too much for them to handle.

Wyoming also happens to be a pretty dry state. It is also relatively vulnerable to fires between the dryness and the strong winds. Wildfires are a fact of life in Wyoming.

Pros

- It features tons of open land
- Plots of land are low cost
- It's great for farming

- The cost of living is low

- There's no income tax

- They are relaxed about homeschooling

- It's suitable for solar power

- It's windy

Cons

- There's not much rain, and many wildfires

Idaho

Idaho might be America's best-kept secret. People already living there and know this don't want anyone else to know it, too. They like it the way it is and don't want to see it getting filled up with city people who are fleeing places like Los Angeles and Portland coming in and ruining it. They will usually treat you well if you don't tell anyone that you are from California.

Pros

- Great farmland and resources to help with farming

- The cost of living is low here

- It offers green energy benefits

- It has many homeschool-friendly options

Cons

- The taxes are high

- There are many natural disasters

A FEW GREAT SPOTS OUTSIDE OF THE US.

The US is great for homesteading and off-grid living, but it is far from the only country you can go to. There are very innovative and adventurous homesteading communities all over the world. Here are a few of our favorites.

Raoul Island, New Zealand

As anyone who has watched *The Lord of the Rings* movies knows, New Zealand is one of the most beautiful countries on Earth. The climate is fantastic, and you can live in paradise. Raoul Island is a small island with a small population. Almost everyone there lives completely or partially off-grid.

Pros

- The off-grid community is already there

- It has an excellent climate

- It features unbelievable scenery

- It has great fishing spots

Cons

- Outside supplies need to be shipped in
- It is not cheap

Lasqueti Island, Canada

Located in Vancouver, British Columbia, Lasqueti Island is home to about 400 people in an off-grid community. If you've never been, Vancouver Island is gorgeous and has everything you need. Vancouver Island has several privately owned islands, so if you are looking to relocate to an excellent off-grid location, you should probably check them out. They are happy to see any visitors who want to check the place out.

Pros

- It features a beautiful environment
- There's great access to fresh water
- There's access to fish
- There's a community of professionals who can help you

Cons

- It can be challenging to get a work permit in Canada
- It's an island, and the only way to leave is by boat or ferry

Khula Dharma, South Africa

Khula Dhamma is an "eco-village," an experiment in green living. People live in updated versions of traditional African huts made with straw and clay, which provide excellent insulation against Africa's hot climate. This community is self-reliant. They produce their own food, electricity, and water.

Pros

- Anyone looking to be green will love this place
- Very knowledgeable bunch of people
- It is inexpensive

Cons

- It may be too rustic for some people
- There is an application process to join the community
- It is very hot

OFF-GRID HOMES

Living in a home you built creates a certain intimacy with your environment that's difficult to put into words. People who have done it understand this even if they've never tried to articulate it.

Imagine you live in a place where every single board is there because you put that board there. Every single nail was hammered into place with your own hands. You know every inch of electrical systems. All the pipes are exactly where you chose to put them. You know how all of these systems work because you couldn't have put them there without knowing it. Better yet, inside of this house are memories of the trials, difficulties, and problems that came along while you were building the home. Each of those memories is a fond one because it is a memory of a challenge you overcame.

The self-made home contains the story of the conquest over challenges and the pride of doing it yourself. You will live inside of a shrine of your own accomplishments. It's not easy to put a price on that.

There are stories of people who are offered large amounts of money to sell their homes to developers who aren't interested in the home itself but are interested in the land for a larger project. You'll often hear these stories of people who are later refusing to sell at any price. They're living in a home they built themselves or built by their parents or their spouse. It's one thing to live in a place for a long time and call it home. It's another thing to create a home.

Fair Warning

Before doing any work on your property, it is vital that you investigate the laws in your state or accounting to make sure you aren't accidentally breaking any. Every place is different, and there's no reliable way to know what you can and cannot do by just using your own common sense. You may need to purchase permits; you may need to use licensed contractors. We would recommend that you reach out to your local government. Call them, or even better, show up in person and ask them directly.

In one example we know of personally, a person dug their own well on a property. There was nothing illegal about that; however, for someone to get a bank loan to purchase the property, they needed it to be inspected. During that inspection, they noticed that the well was not installed by a person with state certification. The banks would not loan money to anyone to purchase the property without the certification by the well digger. The owner would have to destroy the well and replace it with another one or find someone willing to purchase the property upfront in cash. Needless to say, it was a huge disaster.

A mistake like this can mean you waste your money with whatever development you're putting into it; you'll also have to waste money to tear down whatever development you made on the property and then waste even more money doing it the prescribed way. If you accidentally violate an ordinance, you will be fined over and over until the issue is settled. If you can't settle it, the state could take your land from you to pay off the debts from the fines that you can't pay.

Do not make the mistake of assuming you know what the rules are. Unless you are an expert and have a career developing in that area, you must double-check everything.

Cabin or House

It's the most obvious living situation, and that's why it's the first one. This is going to be the option that most people will go with if they plan on staying on the property long-term. Houses are not easy projects, as any homeowner will tell you. When you add on the additional challenges of off-grid living, that means there will be a few other considerations to be mindful of.

Building a cabin has a lot of rewards, though. If you have a family, you will need a place big enough for all of them. If you are laying down roots and really trying to start a life somewhere, this is a good choice. Building a cabin is a sensible choice if you are simply trying to improve the land so that you can rent out your property for Airbnb, small rentals, or eventually sell it.

If you have a big family and need a house, build a house. If it's just you, and you are starting small, don't feel like you need to jump into this right away. If you don't need a house, don't get one until you do.

In some rare cases, you might renovate an older place and retrofit it to work off-grid. This can be harder than just building a new place from scratch. A lot of off-grid resources are most efficient when they are integrated with the house. It's difficult to build something like a radiant heat floor if the floor is already built. Some old houses might be great candidates for renovation, but I'd recommend against it unless you really know what you are doing.

You may want to pay to have a house built or build some of it yourself and hire contractors for other parts. You may not feel qualified to lay a foundation or install an electrical system. If you are a DIY kind of person and you have the time to do the work yourself, it can be a great experience. If you are an experienced contractor, you can just continue to the next chapter because you probably already know exactly what you're going to build.

Yurt

There's always a yurt for the homesteader who wants to live a more old-fashioned and primitive lifestyle. Not everyone wants to keep all the luxuries and indulgences of modern civilization—many people would like to get away from those things. These are small, one-room buildings. Some people will build several on their property, so everyone living there has their own.

These can be very nice and well done. Yurts are very affordable, cozy, and charming. Yurts are not always great if you want a lot of privacy from other people you share the property with. They are also a project that is doable for the layperson. A house is a lot, but a nice yurt is within reach of someone who isn't a pro but would like to make their own home.

Vehicle

Some people like to live in a vehicle. This is a neat option if you don't like staying around in one place for a long time. If you are in a position in life where you like to travel, you can bring a lot of your home with you. Maybe your land is where you call home, but you move around enough that it just makes sense to live in a home with wheels and an engine. You can have a power and water system waiting for you when you come home.

Living in a vehicle doesn't always mean living in a camper. There is a large community that likes to refurbish and retrofit large vehicles to live in them. This could mean something as small as a van, but people have gone as far as refurbishing former ambulances with excellent suspension systems for traversing difficult mountainous areas. Some people have fixed up vehicles that are out of service or retired school buses and rebuilt them into serviceable homes.

There's a tremendous amount of interest in creativity in this lifestyle. Do an Internet search for "van life," and you'll see how popular this trend is, especially with young people.

Shipping Container

It's more common than you may realize, but people have built homes and even larger compounds out of shipping containers—those large rectangular boxes made of corrugated steel that they used to ship goods across the ocean.

If you search on the Internet for many of these things, you might be very impressed with what you find. People have designed remarkably modern and interesting homes by stacking containers and welding them together. They look a lot nicer than we are describing them, and obviously, a lot of work is put into achieving that. There's also been a recent surplus of shipping containers after the COVID-19 pandemic, so getting them now is cheaper than ever.

One technique is to bury the container mostly with dirt with one end of it open. This essentially looks like a hill with a door on the side of it, like a hobbit's home you would see in *The Lord of the Rings*. The drawback here is that you will need a heavy machine to move that much dirt, and you will not have any windows because it is essentially underground. On the plus side, it feels kind of cool, and it has fantastic insulation. When you are mostly underground, you essentially use a geothermal conditioning system that keeps your home warmer and colder in the summer.

Micro Home aka Tiny House

Micro homes are a strange and adorable trend. These are exactly what they sound like: They are super small and very efficiently organized—and very cheap—homes. You can buy a lot of them almost entirely put together. Think of them as recreational vehicles without wheels and much nicer overall.

People have also taken tiny houses and built tiny house communities. They are small enough to be easily taken to even tiny plots of land. People who live in these are often off-grid and rely on a lot of solar and wind power and rainwater. If you can comfortably fit your life inside a New York apartment, you can live in a tiny house. This is a really great option for someone young and single, but definitely not an option for people with families who need space.

KEY CHAPTER TAKEAWAYS

- **Lesson #1: Your Location Means Everything**

Your chosen location determines your lifestyle. It will shape your access to water, soil, and other resources. It will also determine the laws in that area on how you can access water, electricity, heating, cooling, and your nutrition. There are many factors to consider that will help you decide where you want to live.

- **Lesson #2: The Perfect Location For You**

Living off-grid requires you to have many responsibilities, so you need to be someone who likes to stay busy with tasks each day, takes the initiative to learn, loves nature, strives to be healthy and fit, and is committed to making things work. Decide whether this kind of lifestyle is the right choice for you.

- **Lesson #3: The Best US States For Living Off-Grid**

Take on your journey step-by-step, no matter how small. Plan an ideal situation for yourself and be patient as you take on new projects little by little. Not everything has to be perfect overnight. Things take time; your projects don't have to and shouldn't be the end-all immediately. Build slowly and carefully, and do things at your own pace.

- **Lesson #4: The Types of Off Grid Homes**

To have an off-grid mentality, you need a perfect balance of confidence and pessimism. You must be completely prepared for everything, anticipate possible setbacks, emergencies, and disasters, and make the necessary arrangements to prepare for them. You must always be confident in your abilities to make things work and also anticipate any unfortunate situation.

THE NEXT BEST STEP FOR YOU

Reading and learning about all of this at once can be overwhelming, especially for beginners. There can also be growing pressure on yourself when you start to look for your future home. You might be second-guessing despite researching thoroughly. But you don't have to do things on your own. With us, you can do things step-by-step and be sure of your decisions as we guide you along in your journey. Book a call with us today and make your dreams possible!

OFF GRID LOCATION CHECK-IN EXERCISE

Before we proceed with the rest of the book, let's first explore where you are right now in your Off Grid Journey.

Below, rate yourself on a scale of one to five on how accurate the statements are for you—a score of one means "not accurate," and a score of five means "very accurate."

After you have rated yourself according to the statements, add the sum total of your scores, then read "What Your Score Really Means" to determine the outcome of your results.

Check-in Statement	Rating
I have begun researching locations for my off-grid home.	
I know what kind of off-grid home I want to live in.	

I have chosen the location for my off-grid home.	
I know the kind of climate I prefer for my location.	
I have chosen whether I'll build or buy a house.	
I have a budget plan for my future home.	
I am aware of the laws and regulations of the location I want to live in.	
I have applied the factors in my decisions for my off-grid location.	
I am aware of the tax laws in my chosen location.	
I am aware of the cost of living in my chosen location.	
TOTAL SCORE:	

WHAT YOUR SCORE REALLY MEANS

Score: 0 - 15

Lack of Information is Holding You Back

Choosing your location for your future home is one of the most challenging parts when starting this venture. It can be a lot of pressure knowing that your choice will be your home for years to come. Not to mention, it's not cheap, especially when there's already a house built.

You need to ensure you've got everything in order before purchasing your own home. Not being sure about your choices mostly happens when you don't have enough information on the subject, so gathering enough can help you make the correct decisions. Knowing all of your options will make the decision-making process smoother.

Score: 16 - 30

Start Setting Milestones

You've researched enough and know the ropes, but you still don't feel ready to officially buy the lot. Or perhaps you're double thinking about the design of your home. When this happens, setting milestones for yourself as you plan is best.

Create a milestone for completing your research process, choosing a location, or even building your house. This can help you look to the future and know what's in store for you.

Score: 31+

Time to Start Searching for Your Future Home

You have mastered the researching phase, and you're well aware of where you want to be. Now it's time to take a step further and actually buy the lot. There may be a few issues that will come up, such as it not being the right time for you, the need to save up more money, or certain conflicts with work or other people.

It's this time that you should reevaluate everything. Take note of your ideal situation and compare it to what's possible at the moment. As you go on, your expectations can be in line with what can work, and you'll finally reach your goals.

CHAPTER 3: OFF-GRID WATER SYSTEM

In Chapter three, you will read about an extensive list of various water systems when you live off-grid, their different advantages and disadvantages, and how you can set them up yourself.

In the city, when you turn the faucet to wash your hands, bathe, or drink, you expect water to come forth automatically. You know it will come because that's the way things are set up where you live. Access to clean water in your home is a sure thing. However, collecting water will be an everyday part of your routine in other places far away from the city. And many times, clean water is very scarce.

In the Sahara desert, some women wake up before dawn each day to make their journey to collect water. Against the arid and brutal heat, they trudge on for miles until they reach the only nearby place with available water.

They then collect it by lowering and lifting their buckets into the holes in the ground. They become heavy with water but keep it until they're finished. The water is often not even treated, as they don't have access to water filters made by modern technology.

In the wilderness, where bodies of water aren't always accessible, survivors have to collect water from plants or by digging in the ground. Unlike in the city, they can't just expect water to be available when they wake up in the morning. The water here also isn't sure to be clean, so filtering it somehow needs to be practiced.

It's a constant part of their schedule each day because, without water, they can't survive. Many of us have experienced what it's like to have a water shortage. We realize simple things like taking a shower or making tea were things we might have taken for granted.

That's why when you start living off-grid, you'll learn about the realities of collecting, cleaning, and maintaining your water systems. As you read this chapter, you'll learn about the various water systems you can choose from and how to set them up. You'll soon be ready to take on these projects and have a life as comfortable as you can imagine!

In centuries before us, in ancient times, people had to provide basic survival needs for themselves. One main thing they needed was water. Humans are made of 80% water. The average time we can live without it is at most three short days.

Nowadays, many technological advancements and discoveries have made our lives infinitely easier and more prolonged. Still, many of the systems we use today originated hundreds of years ago from our ancestors, who have brought down their knowledge upon us. One piece of knowledge they have taught us is rainwater harvesting. Rainwater harvesting is one way of collecting clean and drinkable water that we still use now!

While it's unknown which civilization performed it first, there is evidence of who practiced it. For example, there's a deep history of rainwater harvesting in the Middle East. The timeline begins in 2000 B.C., when people collected water from the hillside and stored them in Cisterns.

In ancient India, enormous reservoirs were developed to store rainwater! They still practice rainwater harvesting as systems have been built on top of their homes. In Northern America, they collected rainwater from the natural shape of the mountain and the water that would fall from it.

You see, as far back as ancient times, this has been practiced to supply everyone with water, one of the crucial things humans need. It's a tried and true system that has worked for centuries, and especially with our technology now, we can ensure our water is even safer than ever before.

According to the United States Environmental Protection Agency (EPA), the average American family uses 300 gallons of water a day. That isn't a typo. That's 300. Seventy percent (210 gallons) of that water is used inside the home and breaks down as follows ("How We Use Water," 2018):

- Toilet (24 percent)
- Shower/bath (20 percent)
- Faucets (19 percent)
- Washing clothes (17 percent)
- Leaks in the house (12 percent)
- Other (8 percent)

The other 30 percent (90 gallons) is used outdoors for washing cars and watering lawns. Needless to say, we use a lot of water.

That number can be cut down dramatically if you are responsible and conscientious. However, even if you can manage to cut that number in half, you still need a lot of water.

At a bare minimum, you'll want 500 gallons of water on hand at any one time. That's water that's already been pumped or collected and stored in a cistern or tank. If you can get more than 1,000 gallons and safely store them, that will make your life much easier. Storing water is crucial for survival and can also be important for other systems your house uses, such as heating.

CLEANING

Before we even get started on collecting water, we must talk about getting clean water.

Clean water is a serious problem in many parts of the world. Poor access to water, or water contamination, is a tragedy in the developing world. For most of human history, finding a reliable source of clean drinking water was very difficult and crucial. This is why ancient cities were always built on rivers for fresh water.

Water straight out of the ground or a pond will not be clean. It will have mud, clay, and a lot of other gross stuff you don't want to drink. Wherever you get your water from, you will need to include a filtration system—that includes rainwater. Water captured in barrels still probably touched a roof and gutter to be collected. And still, water in a barrel is a breeding ground if it isn't treated.

The most significant risk is any form of contamination by microorganisms. If you ingest these, they can seriously mess up your guts. Water can also be contaminated by gas or contaminants leaking into the soil.

Do not drink unfiltered water. Water contains all kinds of microscopic organisms that will seriously harm you and potentially kill you.

Simply boiling water kills many different types of contaminants but not all. Most viruses of the bacteria won't survive as they boil. Others can survive and can only be killed at a very high temperature, usually requiring a pressure cooker. Boiling may be a good enough solution for short-term survival, but boiling water in a pressure cooker is not a good long-term system.

Modern filters are so tight that the gaps in the mesh are measured in fractions of a micrometer. This means most microscopic particulates and organisms cannot get through it. It's also a great way of moving any kind of junk in your water. They usually contain a mix of ceramic and carbon, the same thing they use in the water filters that attach to your sink or use in a pitcher. Filters will need to be replaced periodically. Consult the instructions of any filter you use.

For your rain barrels, you might want to use tablets. Water purifying tablets kill most biological invaders. Tablets usually use iodine, chlorine, or sodium, so you must be careful not to overtreat the water. You do not want to be consuming too much of the stuff that cleans the water. Purifying tablets also can't remove any harmful particulates, such as heavy metals.

Ultraviolet light can purify water by killing microbes' ability to produce. Normal exposure to light can recontaminate the water. Light-treated water must be used shortly after cleaning or stored in a lightproof location.

If you have no water access, you have probably chosen the wrong place to live. If for some reason, you find yourself in a position where you only have access to saltwater, solar-powered desalination is an option.

In short, to get safe water, you will have one or more solutions to handle both biological and nonorganic junk.

RAIN

Rain is free, easy, and clean. It falls from the sky, and all you have to do is catch it before the earth drinks it. Setting up a series of rain barrels is the simplest way to do this.

You want to use any large surface area as a way to collect. Easy examples are the roof of your home and solar panels. The water can be caught using gutters and delivered into barrels. Just leaving a bunch of barrels out in the yard will not be very effective if you want to maximize the space to capture.

As mentioned earlier in this chapter, barrel water needs to be treated. You absolutely do not want algae or mosquitoes finding a home inside of it.

Rainwater is great, but it will not be enough for you. If you live in a very rainy environment and it's just you, maybe you can get away with it—probably not, though. For most people, especially those with children, rain barrels are a vital part of the water system, but they are not enough themselves. Rain barrels are supplemental. They won't be the most important water source.

If you can, have the rainwater diverge directly into one of your main tanks. If you can't do that, you can manually add the water directly to the tank if you don't mind a little bit of heavy lifting. Rainwater can also just be used as a gravity shower.

In the winter, your rainwater is now snow water. If you heat it up, it will serve the same function. It's also much easier to collect because it's all over the place, and you can just scoop it up.

Believe it or not, harvesting rainwater is actually illegal in some places. Make sure you won't get a fine for catching the water from the sky.

WELLS

If you're going to be living somewhere, you want a permanent, stable, and reliable water source—that means a well. For your main water source, digging a well is by far your best bet. Rain is fine if there's a supplement. Creeks and ponds might not be available or legal to take from. Delivery is fine temporarily, but it's not a permanent solution.

Shallow Well or Pump Well?

If there is water high enough, you may be lucky in that you can dig a shallow well. Basically, you need to get an excavator to dig out a big hole in the ground, about ten feet in diameter and around 18 or 20 feet in depth. If you're finding water at that depth, you are in luck. I'll keep saying it: Check your laws. Some pumps that go deeper than a precise number of feet are regulated. Yes, the laws are that finicky.

Once you have a hole, you can install the pipe, valve, and pump and run the pipe up over the top. Then, fill in the rest with gravel, then cover with dirt.

If you are feeling really rustic, you need water now but don't have electricity yet; or if you want a second, minor well, you can always use a lever hand pump—very old-fashioned but very effective for small amounts of water. Not a great way to get water for your whole house, but it's excellent as an intermediary step or a supplementary system.

DEEP WELL

One thing that's been a problem with settling new land is finding locations to dig a well. It wasn't that long ago that con artists were making money using dowsing rods, wandering between the town, and promising they could detect places that were good for a well. Then he'd take their money and disappear before the people who hired them could realize their mistake.

Any piece of land that you want to dig a well on, you should investigate ahead of time. It would be a good idea to reach out and talk to the neighbors first. See if anyone else nearby has dug their own well. If none of them have, you might be able to speak with folks in the city about any records they have of natural resources. If you are going to need a well, you should use land where you are likely to find water.

Digging a well blind is extremely risky. If no other wells are nearby and you don't have good information on the water table, you are firing blind.

You may be able to take a relatively shallow well with just an auger and get very lucky. However, in some places, you need to dig and install pipes that are hundreds of feet down. Every single one of those feet costs a lot of money. Maybe you get lucky, and you find water 40 feet down. Maybe you don't get lucky and drill down 300 feet and still find nothing. The people who dig the well get paid whether they find water or not.

A well is probably your best source of water, but if you are not careful, you can end up spending a tremendous amount of money with no benefit. So be very careful.

Digging a well may be one of the most expensive projects to get your off-grid home up and running. However, on the plus side, adding a well will greatly raise the property value. As long as you did it with a company following all the rules and licenses, the value added to the land should pay for itself if you ever decide to sell.

SPRINGS, RIVERS, AND CREEKS

If you find a river or creek on your land, you may feel like you have an excellent water supply. We hate to break it to you, but many states do not allow you to draw water out of creeks, rivers, and ponds crossing through your land. That makes it illegal to draw water from a naturally occurring source. This is doubly true out west. Where water is especially scarce, they have appropriative water rights.

That creak, stream, or river you have somewhere potentially crosses through somebody else's lawn on its destination to some other larger body of water. It would be seriously uncool to interfere with that stream as across as someone else's land. That's why you can't just build a dam and divert the water in another direction. That messes with someone else's property.

If you were grabbing some 100 gallons a year, you might not get caught, but we cannot recommend breaking state law to get water when there are other ways to do it. You may have to enjoy the calming and serene bliss of the water, but tragically, you won't be able to take a shower with it.

DELIVERY AND PICKUP

In survival training, they will teach you that you can go three hours without shelter, three days without water, and three weeks without food. We need to upend that rule a little bit on our priorities. To get water, we need to pump. To get a pump working, we'll need electricity, so electricity is actually more important than water.

If you're developing an area with a hill, you can make things easier by putting water cisterns on top of the hill and running a line to your house, trenching it, and burying it underground. Natural gravity will give you natural water pressure without requiring any extra electricity.

When you first start your off-grid home, it may be a while before you can get access to your own water. You may be reliant on water from outside. If you have tanks set up and buried, with valves and pumps installed and pipes going to your home, you can hire a truck to deliver water and fill up your tanks. If not, you can go to the store, pick up as much as you need, and drive it back.

This is not a good long-term solution to your water problems. This is just costing you gasoline and time, plus the water is more expensive than if you were on the grid. You can rely on this kind of water supply for a short time while getting your permanent water system fully operational. Also, if there's some kind of problem down the road and you need to repair your system, or something gets funky, you can get the water delivered if it's the last resort.

We only include it in this book because, realistically, you will be using delivered water for a short period at the start of your off-grid homesteading.

STORAGE

Water needs to be stored. You won't be pumping water every time you turn on a faucet. Water is pumped and stored in tanks as needed. Your indoor water is drawn from the tanks. The bigger the tanks, the more water you have at the ready. You want large volumes of it ready to go.

Like everything else, if you want to be prepared and have more than you need, get it now because you might need it later.

Tanks and cisterns should be stored underground. After just a few feet into the earth, the ground is cool but not frozen. This is important because in the summer, the place under the ground will not begin cooking near water and making it 90 degrees. It won't freeze or burst in the winter and become impossible to use.

Any kind of pump system will also need to be underground, including the valve. Like the water, you do not want the mechanics of getting the water out of your pump to freeze—that would be a severe disaster. How much water you'll need and how big your tank is will depend on your personal needs, but we always recommend getting more than you need just to be safe.

Water collected from rain can always be added to your tanks to top them off and give your pump a break.

KEY CHAPTER TAKEAWAYS

- **Lesson #1: The Importance of Clean Water**

Once you begin collecting your water, you'll need to find a way to clean it. Ensuring the cleanliness of your water will prevent many diseases you can get from unfiltered water. Knowing how to filter and prevent such things will allow you and your family to stay healthy as you live off the grid.

- **Lesson #2: Different Ways to Collect Water**

The main systems you can use to collect water as you live off-grid are rain barrels, cisterns, and various kinds of wells. Some of these you can set up on your own, but others may need assistance from licensed professionals.

- **Lesson #3: Laws & Bodies of Water**

Many times, bodies of water near your off-grid home will have laws prohibiting you from collecting from them. Knowing the laws in your area and ensuring that the body of water is safe to take your water from will make things much smoother.

- **Lesson #4: Delivery & Pickup of Your Water**

In the beginning stages of living off-grid, you won't automatically have collected water at your disposal. Knowing how to order and pick up enough water for you and your family will help you prepare for the coming weeks ahead.

- **Lesson #4: Storing Your Water**

Once you collect your water, you must find a way to store it so you won't waste a drop and can use it in the long run. Some ways to store them are in your rain barrels, cisterns, and tanks.

A Hands-On Approach to Your Learning

We know there are different types of learners, and reading and researching may not be as effective for some people. That's why we encourage you to come and book a call with us as soon as possible.

You'll reach your goals faster than you could alone and accelerate your learning to finally be independent. Your journey doesn't have to be so confusing and complicated because we'll be your guide every step of the way.

Off Grid Water Reliance Check-in Exercise

Before we proceed with the rest of the book, let's first explore where you are right now in your Off Grid Journey.

Below, rate yourself on a scale of one to five on how accurate the statements are for you -- a score of one means "not accurate," and a score of five means "very accurate."

After you have rated yourself according to the statements, add the sum total of your scores, then read "What Your Score Really Means" to determine the outcome of your results.

Check-in Statement	Rating
I am still reliant on the city's water systems.	
I have selected a water system for collecting water.	

I know **where** to collect water and how to clean it.	
I have a budget plan for my water collection system.	
I know the primary systems I can use to collect water.	
I know the laws in my area and ensure that the body of water is safe to take.	
I know what to build for a steady running water supply in my home.	
I know how to order and pick up enough water to help me prepare for the coming weeks ahead.	
I know the advantages and disadvantages of each water system option.	
I know the proper way to store water so I can use it in the long run.	
I have a working, foolproof, dependable water system in my home.	
TOTAL SCORE:	

What Your Score Really Means

Score: 0 - 15
Reviewing Stage is Needed

With this score, you might have difficulty understanding how water management works. The function of water systems and how to set them up will be crucial because you'll need it daily. Clean, running water will allow you to do your daily tasks, cook, and hydrate, all of which are needed for your survival. Since it's all up to you, you have to be more hands-on and review further on the things you have to know.

Score: 16 - 30

Ready to Choose Your Water System

You are well on your way to really getting the hang of things. Once you finally choose your water system, you're one step closer to a more self-sufficient life. Now, your job is to set everything aside and decide how you want your things to be.

Score: 31+

Prepared to Set Things up

You have already done what's necessary to overcome the lack of know-how for certain things. Now, it's time for you to take the next step. After you've chosen a system to set up for your home, it's time to review how you will do so.

For some water systems, you won't need an extra pair of hands to set things up, but when building specific ones, such as a well, you'll have to navigate what you can or cannot do.

CHAPTER 4: GENERATING OFF-GRID POWER

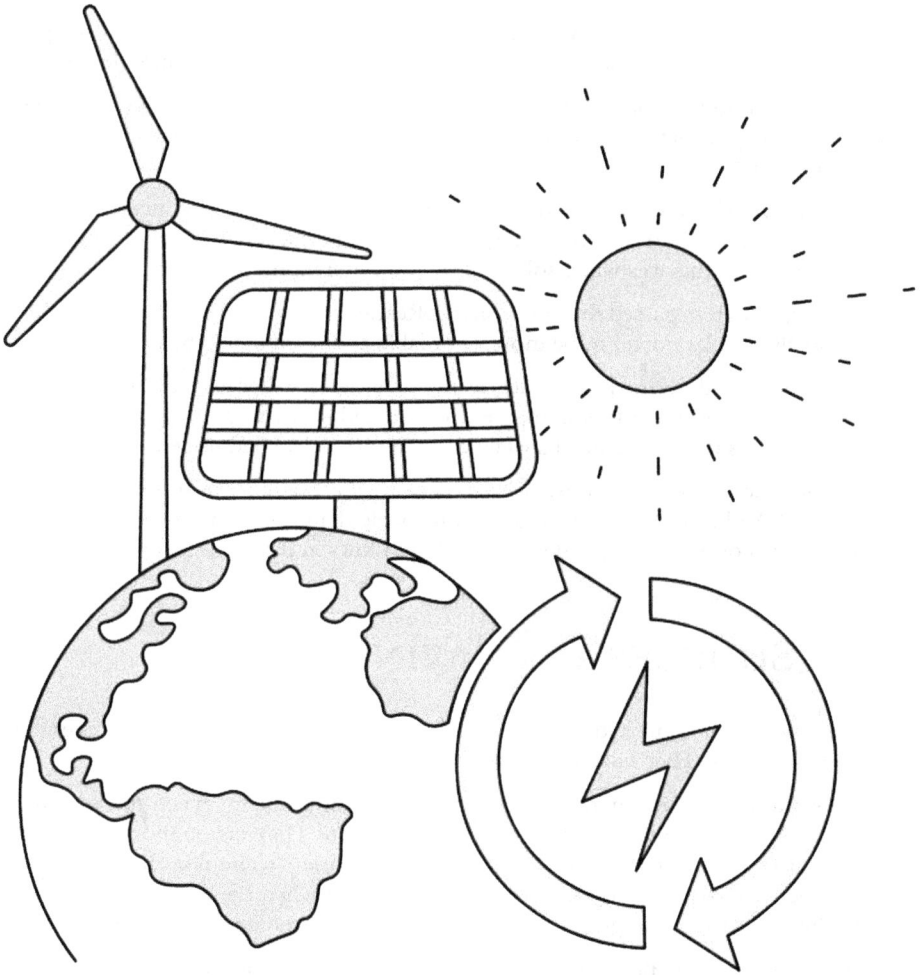

Chapter four lays out information on one of the most complex systems for living off-grid: electricity. You'll learn about the various types of power sources for electricity, how solar, wind, and geothermal power works, and how to set them up yourself.

As centuries passed, we can now experience the splendor that this discovery brought. We can live in the comfort and privilege of having a warm home, using our daily gadgets, and having light available whenever we need it!

Imagine a home without any power at all! Not only would it be a pain, but you wouldn't be able to use any of the appliances or gadgets you need daily for chores and work. When you live off-grid, you'll need to learn how to set up your power systems. Living comfortably and off the grid is possible with more knowledge gained. Throughout this chapter, you'll learn exactly what you need to do to power your future home.

Solar energy has been used by our ancestors as far back as five BC. One of its first ways to be used was to light fires through magnification with glass.

North American Anasazi people even practiced keeping their homes warm by designing their homes to face the sun, which today would be called a passive solar architecture design.

Many discoveries about solar energy took place during the 16th and 17th centuries. But everything truly started taking shape when Edmond Becquerel discovered the Photovoltaic effect or light energy in 1839.

Many new inventions were created afterward until 1954, when Bell Laboratory finally created silicon solar cells that could transform sunlight into electricity! While it could only power small appliances at that time, this was when solar energy was revolutionized.

Decades later, Congress passed the Solar Energy Research, Development and Demonstration Act of 1974 to allow solar power to be more affordable and feasible for the masses.

Nowadays, more and more people are using solar energy because of how much of a sustainable and clean resource it is compared to our traditional ways of getting energy. It is important because it's one of the most sustainable ways to collect and use energy.

Thanks to our ancestors and scientists who have made this possible, solar energy is even more affordable today! And now, living off grid is more viable than ever. With solar energy, we'll be able to have all the comforts that modern technology allows in more sustainable ways!

POWER SOURCES AND SAVING

Renewable energy has come a long way but isn't a fully mature technology. Like everything in life, there are trade-offs. They have pros, and they have cons.

Solar and wind power can generate a tremendous amount of energy when the sun and wind are at their peak. This is great except for one big problem: They create more energy than is needed. The surplus energy can't be stored safely because battery technology hasn't been able to keep pace. When the solar panels aren't catching the sun or when the wind isn't blowing, they produce nothing. We need energy when we need it, not just when nature provides it.

Living off-grid means living on an electrical budget. On a municipal scale, this means that green energy still has to be supplemented with other energy, be it nuclear or coal. On a small scale, you can be flexible enough to make it work. You will want to get a reasonable estimate of how much energy you need. If you can get an estimate of how much energy you are using now, you can get a sense of how much energy production you will need in your off-grid home.

1,000–1,500W is probably enough juice for your needs, but everyone's needs differ.

The power source you use will depend on your environment. The more you can mix your energy sources, the better. If one isn't generating, another one might be able to make up the difference. The diversity of energy is reliable energy.

Naturally produced energy is about living on nature's schedule. When it offers wind or sun, you take it while you can get it. If you are using naturally produced power from wind and solar energy, you are living on an electrical budget. You have to regulate your own energy use because you can just use as much as you want and pay a bill for it later.

One way of handling this is by using the power when you have the power. This is called "opportunity usage" and is a very effective way to maximize your power. Schedule all your heavy electrical activities for when the sun is up, and the wind is blowing, and there will be no wasted energy. If you have a washing machine and dryer and a sunny day, that would be an excellent time to do your laundry.

SOLAR

Solar energy is cheaper and more available now than ever before. It's so common that it's no longer unusual to see solar arrays attached to the roofs of someone's home. Solar panels are made of crystalline silicon wafers. Contact with sunlight causes electrons to move about inside of them, and this flow of electrons is what generates an electrical current.

Big solar farms optimize their energy to follow the sun by turning the panels automatically to always face the sun and have the optimal angle with maximum coverage of the surface area of the panels. This is exactly how sunflowers operate—they always move to face the sun so they can get as much sunlight as possible.

Not all solar panels are equal. Some people simply lay them flat on the ground—that is the least effective way of catching the sun. It'll be great and high noon during the summer when the sun is directly above it, but it will be increasingly useless as the sun goes down.

Higher-end models can do what those major industrial solar panels do and follow the sun. They are definitely more expensive, but they may be worth the initial investment if you can get more juice out of them and optimize your array.

Most people find that installing panels on the roof of their home is the smartest option depending on how they face the sun. Many people set up arrays on towers about the property, in areas without any shade or trees blocking them. Very often, the best place to put your solar array is in the garden for the same reasons. It's an open space with lots of sunshine.

You can't make a solar panel system without some electrical skills. If you know something about wiring up an electrical system or are willing to learn, you can do it yourself. However, it can be risky if you are inexperienced. Faulty craftsmanship can damage some of the systems and cost you money and time.

Building your own system takes planning and research. As stated many times in this book, always check out your local regulations. Some places require permits or official qualifications.

Solar panels also need to be weatherproofed. After they are put up and jointed together, they need to be sealed so that water and moisture do not get into them. Make sure that any panels you purchase are from a reputable supplier and manufacturer. Getting cheap panels from an untrustworthy supplier could result in a fire. Look around. If something seems so cheap that it's too good to be true, it is. Safety first.

You can build solar panels from scratch out of individual solar cells if you like. It's not too difficult. You start by creating a backing for the panel. You can use a wooden board, and you will need to drill holes in the right place so that wires from each cell can pass through the back. They are then wired together using a soldering iron. They should be attached to your backing individually so they can be removed individually. If a single solar cell is damaged, it should be relatively easy to remove the single damaged cell and replace it without having to replace the entire thing.

A solar panel by itself doesn't do anything without an electrical system. You need to pair your panels with an inverter to turn the direct current (DC) into an alternating current (AC). Nearly everything you use requires AC power. Running DC into that stuff will not work.

Before you even begin designing your system, you should probably get a sense of how much power you will need. Look at your current electrical bill, and you might be able to get an estimate of how much juice you are using. Then, look at weather reports to see how many days of sunshine you get on average in the area that you are building. With a little bit of math, you should be able to get a sense of what the scope of your solar system needs to look like.

For beginners, we recommend that you purchase solar panel kits that come with all the instructions included and all of the tools necessary to build your solar system. Good kits also include racking and a means of mounting your system. If you want to do it yourself but don't really know how, these kits are definitely a wonderful option.

Wrecking refers to installing it on either the ground or onto the roof. If you are using an RV, then you will need to mount it on that. Whichever method you use, these must be very secure; you don't want them falling off or getting blown away by the gusty wind. Getting your solar panels from the same place you get your racking supplies might be a good idea to guarantee they will fit together. Even though some companies promise compatibility, these things can sometimes be like blue jeans. The size on the label says one thing, but when you actually try it on, you find it isn't quite what was promised.

Working with a professional who is a trained electrician with expertise in solar panel installation will likely be your best bet. They know all the laws and regulations, they are experts in their field, and they will probably get it right the first time. If you are a DIY person who knows a little bit of that electricity and is willing to learn a lot more, this can be a great project for you to take on yourself. Letting a professional deal with it is a good call if you don't feel up to it.

Catching the sun won't be reliable for those living in places like the Pacific Northwest of America or Scotland. You can keep adding panels, but adding other energy sources is better.

WIND

The wind is a great option if you live out in the open in a windy place like Argentina, Perth, or Wyoming. If you live deep in the woods, you might not get enough wind to make it worth your while. Trees do a great job of breaking up the wind and sheltering you from hurricanes and dangerously forceful winds. Unfortunately, it also means you can't get wind power.

Wind turbines are commercially available, but they aren't cheap. Some can generate as much as 3,000W—emphasis on CAN. Like solar power, just because the box says it can generate a large wattage doesn't mean it will. Nature makes that decision.

A lot of areas do not like the look of windmills, and regulate them. Like everything else, check the laws to ensure you're allowed to have them. Windmills also need to be mounted on polls. Usually, higher is better, as there is less obstruction from your buildings, hills, and trees. Around 20 feet should do the trick in most cases.

GEOTHERMAL

Geothermal is a very cool option with one major drawback: Getting it up and running can be very pricey.

Geothermal energy is not actually producing electrical power. It just makes heating and cooling easier and more efficient.

Geothermal works by drilling a deep hole in the earth and running water through it. The deeper into the earth you go, the less affected it is by the temperatures on the surface. In effect, the temperature is stable.

When it is ferociously hot outside, the temperature deep in the earth is cooler. When it is intensely cold outside, the temperature in the earth is warmer.

The more you want to change the temperature, the more energy you need. It takes more heat to make ice into a gas than it does to turn liquid water into a gas.

Geothermal works by splitting that amount of energy by meeting your energy need halfway. If you need to cool things down, the geothermal temperature gets you halfway from hot to cold. If you need it warmer, then it's the same thing.

It is very simple, practical, and, most importantly, reliable.

This is highly recommended. It doesn't provide electricity, but it makes your electrical systems much more efficient for heating and cooling your home and water.

MICRO-HYDRO

This is a very interesting option if your spot has running water. Unlike solar and wind, a moving river or creek is always moving. Depending on the time of year, you'll get more or less power, but it's always there for you if you need it.

Reach out to the Geological Survey or Department of Agriculture. They may have data on the speed and force of the water moving through your property. Hydropower might not be worth your time if it isn't strong enough. If your water source does produce enough force, like every other improvement on your land, you should contact whatever local department is in charge of energy or natural resources and ask them about the rules for diverting water.

If you have a green light for those two items, you'll need a generator, turbine, and piping. Consider yourself lucky because this is not an option available to most people living off the grid.

GAS-POWERED GENERATOR

A generator isn't anyone's first choice, but it's important to include. It uses gasoline—which is expensive and a pollutant—it's loud, and it smells bad. That said, you're going to want one.

You may need a generator to get by while getting yourself set up. You will need something until your other power sources are up and running.

It's important to have a generator in case of emergencies. Even if you seldom need it, you'll be very happy to have it when you do. As we discussed earlier, several overlapping redundancies are crucial. You'll want a generator just in case. If you accidentally leave your keys in your truck overnight and drain your car battery, you will be very grateful to have a generator.

Important note: Gasoline goes bad. Gas is perishable. It has a shorter life span than you might realize. If you have a spare plastic tank of gas, you will need to change it out periodically. Pure gas that is properly stored can last six months. Gas blended with ethanol lasts three months, so keep this in mind. You don't want to fill a tank with bad gas.

There are options for petroleum-based stabilizers to add to gas, which will extend its life to one to three years.

If your gas looks too dark or you see any sludge in it, it is old, and you can't use it. Putting old or contaminated gas can ruin the machine you're trying to power.

STORAGE

Energy storage is going to be necessary because the wind won't always be blowing, and the sun won't always be shining. To store the energy, we have two main options.

The obvious answer is batteries. There are lots of options, and not all batteries are created equal. You can get heavy acid batteries, the kind that is used in golf carts. Those are a fine option and relatively cheap, although they are heavy and filled with acid, and you do not want to tip them over because they are full of liquid. You can also find lithium batteries, the same type used in your cell phones. These are cheaper but also more expensive and often have less capacity.

Obviously, you'll need an electrical system to build these batteries and pull power from them when needed into any other electricity you are using in the home.

Battery storage is measured in ampere-hours. That means a 100-ampere hour battery will give you 100 amps for one hour... sort of. Batteries also have a natural discharge rate. This is called Peukert's law, which complicates the math a little. Batteries have different discharge rates that will also affect how much juice you get out of them. People who know a lot about this will check batteries for Peukert's exponents.

The discharge rate can also be affected by the temperature and the battery's age. This is all complicated stuff, and it actually isn't that important. You don't need to calculate the exact amounts of storage you need. You need to get a rough estimate of what you need and then add on a little bit extra just to be safe.

Energy can also be stored in water. Water is very conductive of energy. This isn't energy you can convert into electricity, but you are effectively storing thermal energy by heating water. When the sun is shining, and you are pulling in a lot of power from your solar arrays, this is a great time to channel some of that energy into your water heater. Tanks with hot water will stay hot for a while. As we discussed, you will be pulling more energy in than you need at that time and more than you can store for later. Heating your water during the day is the perfect opportunity to store energy in the water.

Key Chapter Takeaways

- **Lesson #1: Off-Grid Power Sources**

Your source for electricity when you live off-grid will be quite different because you'll be relying on renewable energy. Your choice of energy source will also greatly depend on your location's environment and weather conditions.

- **Lesson #2: Saving on Power**

As you live off-grid and rely on renewable energy to power your home, you'll need to make certain adjustments. Because your power source will rely on the wind or sunlight, there will be times when there's more or less power than usual. So regulating your energy according to that will help you make the most out of the power.

- **Lesson #3: The Best Options For Renewable Energy**

There are many sources of energy to power your home. Some of these are solar, wind, geothermal, and micro-hydropower. A gas-powered generator is often used as a backup if ever these fail to give electricity.

- **Lesson #4: Storing Your Power**

Storing your energy is crucial because you won't always have the light or wind to help give power to your home. Using a special and appropriate kind of battery will allow you to enjoy electricity in your home even when the weather conditions don't allow it.

Don't Be Held Back by the Technical Aspects

Powering your off-grid home is a tremendously difficult task. You'll have to research and decide on your power source, learn how to set it up, and have some knowledge on maintenance as well.

For some of us, we could get put off just from realizing the amount of work we'll have to do. But the thing is, you don't have to do it all on your own. Why not get a team of experts who can make things infinitely easier and faster for you?

Book a call with us today to take that burden off your shoulders. Nothing has to hold you back any longer from achieving the lifestyle you want.

OFF GRID POWER SOURCES CHECK-IN EXERCISE

Before we proceed with the rest of the book, let's first explore where you are right now in your Off Grid Journey.

Below, rate yourself on a scale of one to five on how accurate the statements are for you -- a score of one means "not accurate," and a score of five means "very accurate."

After you have rated yourself according to the statements, add the sum total of your scores, then read "What Your Score Really Means" to determine the outcome of your results.

Check-in Statement	Rating
I know about different renewable energy sources.	
I know the different power sources I can choose from to power my off-grid home.	
I have chosen a power source for my off-grid home.	
I have estimated how much power I need for my home.	
I have a budget plan for purchasing and setting up my off-grid power systems.	

I know how I will store my power.	
I am aware of the laws and regulations on off-grid power.	
I have knowledge of ways to save power for living off-grid.	
I know the advantages and disadvantages of each power source option.	
I know what I need to plan and purchase for the different power sources.	
TOTAL SCORE:	

What Your Score Really Means

Score: 0 - 15

Power Your Understanding

Setting up power in your off-grid home is one of the trickiest things to master. Right now, your knowledge of it still needs to be polished, so the best thing to do is go over the chapter again. You should also research the power system you're most interested in.

Score: 16 - 30

Reassess Your Needs

You may have learned nearly everything you need to set up your power system, but you still feel as if you're at a crossroads. When this happens, you need to reassess your needs and what you can do. You might be feeling overwhelmed, and you need to take things step by step. Rethinking the necessities and focusing on those will help you continue without as much confusion.

Score: 31+

Begin to Set Up Your Power System

Now that most of your decisions are set and done, nearly the hardest parts are over. But now, you can use more hands-on experience for this stage in your journey. Since you know the items and resources you need, you can begin setting up your power system. It won't be easy, but knowing how to go about it step-by-step will make things much easier.

CHAPTER 5: OFF-GRID NUTRITION

In chapter five, you'll discover ways to supply yourself with nutrients once you live off-grid, including growing your food, raising livestock, the best foods to stock up on, and ways to preserve and store your sustenance.

You look past your window to the wide splendor of a garden. Your harvest for the year is slowly growing, vivid hibiscus and hollyhocks sway to the wind, and your apple and lemon trees are steadily sprouting hearty fruit.

You take out your tools, put on your boots, and as you step outside, you stroll across the field. The sky is crisp and clear blue. The smell of the air is sweeter from the fragrant flowers dotted along your feet.

You harvest the food that's ready: the potatoes, beans, basil, carrots, and leeks. You realize you have more than enough to eat as you begin thinking about all the recipes you can cook. After tending to your garden, you visit your hens to see freshly laid eggs. You collect each of them and clean up your coop. You plan on making scrambled eggs for breakfast. After you're done with the morning tasks, you admire your own paradise, one you made with your own hands!

This picture of life doesn't have to stay in your imagination because this paradise can be real in a world where food shortages happen. Sometimes people have no way to take care of themselves except to depend entirely on unstable systems.

Knowing how to grow your own food and provide for yourself and your family is one step to complete self-sufficiency. Soon, you'll learn how you can supply yourself with needed nutrients, be prepared, and even have your personal paradise.

We live in an increasingly industrially reliant culture. A culture that relies on fast food, disposable goods, and wasteful materials—a culture that is fast eating itself up. But there's a set of agricultural systems that throw this way of life out of the window. This is *permaculture*, a movement created to promote a sustainable and independent lifestyle.

It all began in the 1970s with ecologists and coworkers Bill Mollison and David Holmgren. They realized the growing damages of the Industrial Revolution and its impact on our culture, so they created permaculture. Through their study, they discovered how nature goes through sustainable cycles without the help of man. They then were able to live in and teach their philosophy to others.

There is also another man, Masanobu Fukuoka, who has slowly built a following in this movement. He endorses a natural way of farming, where you disrupt the soil only to a minimum. Instead of weeding, he chose to flood his fields with water, which helped weaken the weeds. They were trimmed if necessary, but as much as possible, he let them grow.

Another voice in this movement is Ruth Stout, who advocates mulching plants with twigs, pulled weeds, leaves, and more. She also promotes no-till gardening, and many have followed her ideas.

From its humble beginnings, it's evident that permaculture has evolved into a revolutionary change. More people can now learn and apply these revolutionary teachings to create a healthier life for themselves. As we depend more on sustainable agriculture, we'll be more independent from using unreliable sources.

This movement promotes a sustainable lifestyle and also interdependence with community members. As you plan to live off-grid, you can learn infinite lessons from these mentors as you start to grow your own food and become self-sufficient.

Eating seems to be one of the most popular topics. That's for a good reason: People love food. Plus, when you grow your own food, you have a more personal relationship with it. It's one thing to go to the store and pick up a zucchini; it's another thing entirely to grow that zucchini yourself from start to finish, see the final product, and then prepare it and feed it to yourself and other people.

A lot of people are very concerned about their food. What you eat is very important, and if you are especially alert about these things, there is no better way to know what you are eating than to be the person who makes it. Large agricultural corporations have earned themselves a bad reputation due to their practices of using pesticides and genetically modifying their crops. It's no surprise then that organic markets and farmers' markets have become so popular.

GROWING FOOD

Gardening

You're certainly going to want a garden. A garden is a fantastic option if you aren't using a full-scale farming operation. To maximize the value and productivity of that garden, we strongly recommend that you build a greenhouse. Greenhouses are less challenging to make than you might expect and have a few significant effects.

A garden inside of a greenhouse is less vulnerable to animals. If built correctly and securely, you won't have to worry about foxes and rabbits sneaking in and eating your greens.

Plants prefer warmer environments. The greenhouse contains both heat and moisture so that the plants are warm without drying out. The roof and walls protect the plants from the elements. Some plants are very sensitive to heavy rainfall, and several days of bad rain could wreck a garden. Depending on what you are growing ultimately depends on what the optimal temperature is. If you are going to be growing several plants at once, make sure that their optimal temperature overlaps so that all of them can be happy.

You want to keep the greenhouse relatively humid, but try not to break the 90 percent mark. Too much humidity could lead to mold. Likewise, if things get too cold at night, humidity can turn to frost and freeze your plants, so ensure that you are maintaining the heat during the night as well.

Every garden should have a few staple items. For a beginner, it's best to stick with plants that aren't too needy. Since you can maximize the heat and water levels, the greenhouse will extend the natural planting season, and you will be able to get more food in one year than you normally would otherwise.

Vegetables that aren't a terrible amount of work include:

- Any kind of hardy root vegetable, including carrots
- Basil
- Oregano
- Tomatoes
- Onions
- Garlic
- Cucumber
- Zucchini
- Lettuce
- Spinach
- Bell peppers
- Celery

The French chefs reading this book probably noticed that all of the ingredients for mirepoix are present. Many Cajun chefs also noted that the Louisiana variation, "holy trinity," is also included on the list. Needless to say, you know you are off to a good start.

A garden that you plan on living off is a garden that produces all the things that you need to live—that means proteins, fats, antioxidants, and carbohydrates. Skipping out on any of these is not healthy.

If you're making a garden to survive, nutritional values can be the most important thing. Your staples will include:

- Potatoes

- Carrots
- Beans
- Squash
- Tomatoes
- Onions
- Corn

You want to mix and match your garden with foods that take little time to grow and also those that grow quickly. Then you can overlap their cycles and produce a constant set of nourishing plants.

Some of the plants that have a short harvest cycle include:

- Carrots
- Kale
- Spinach
- Beans

All these will grow to full size within one to two months generally. Potatoes can take three to four months if you use a spud from some of your older potatoes.

Vegetables don't last long. As soon as you pick them, their clock starts ticking. If you plan on doing a full harvest so that you can replant all of them, make sure you have a plan to consume them or at least a plan to store them. Effectively storing them will be covered later in this chapter.

If you can, you should also get a few herbs growing. A bit of herb goes a long way, and you can grow most of them easily. Basil, rosemary, sage, parsley, and thyme are all relatively simple and are excellent in food when they are fresh if you haven't tried them before.

The first part of running a garden is learning how to do it and getting it set up. The nice thing about plants is that most of the growing they do doesn't require much help from you. They do all of the work as long as you put them in a good environment with good soil, water, light, and the right temperature.

If you want to get really fancy, you can integrate a greenhouse automation system. This requires a little bit of tactical know-how, but it will save you quite a bit of work in the long run.

By running pipes over your garden with small holes on it, with a time valve, you can have the garden automatically water itself. After the programmed period, water will automatically pump through the pipes and sprinkle the water out of the tiny holes, provided that you put the pipes in the right places. This automatic valve mechanism can be controlled via the computer.

Another way to use computers is by ventilating your greenhouse. The temperature inside the greenhouse can't get too hot. Plants like hot temperatures, but they have their limits. Using a computer to check the temperature and automatically turn on a fan to start ventilating the greenhouse is a great way of letting a machine do the micromanagement for you.

If you have a greenhouse, that's excellent, but if your garden is going to be too large to use in a greenhouse or you don't want a greenhouse for whatever reason, you are going to need to protect your garden from critters that will want to go in there and enjoy your snacks. Putting any kind of fencing around it so that rabbits and deer don't just wander in and enjoy themselves at your expense is necessary.

Raising Animals

Chickens

Chickens are great. Chickens will produce an egg every other day or so. The daily recommended minimum for protein consumption is about 50 grams. An egg contains about six grams of protein. So a breakfast of three eggs will contain about one-third of your daily required protein intake.

For chickens, you will absolutely need to build them a chicken coop. This usually entails an area fenced in with chicken wire with a little indoor home for them to sit comfortably. You can also let them out during the day—they know where their home is and will return. They'll love to look for bugs on your lawn, but you don't want them out all the time because they are delicious treats for predators in the wild.

There is so much support and information out there. There is an increasing interest in raising home chickens or even ducks. You can find lengthy tutorials on how to raise these animals online. Even in places like Detroit, a lot of people have taken up urban farming projects and created chicken coops in the middle of the suburbs. Now is a great time to get into chicken farming on a small scale.

Chickens are very stupid and like to use their water as a bathroom. Change the water to make sure they don't kill themselves like that.

Chickens are great for laying eggs, but let us never forget that chickens are also great to eat. If you are raising organic, free-range chickens, you will get a very different product than what you might be used to at a grocery store. Your chickens will be considerably smaller but also way tastier. The ones you purchase at the store have been given growth hormones to make them huge, they get very little exercise and only "eat" rain. If you don't mind reducing your chicken consumption, you will have some extra tasty chicken as a reward.

A strange fact is that your chickens will seem to spontaneously die sometimes. You won't know why, and you can't afford a chicken autopsy. Don't be surprised when you come to your chicken village and find one of them didn't survive. That's just going to happen.

In any chicken coop, you will want one rooster. You do not want zero roosters, and you do not want two roosters. One rooster is exactly the right amount.

One rooster will be a good defender of the hens. The rooster will step in if anyone tries to mess with their hens. If there are zero roosters, the hens are out of luck.

If you put two roosters next to each other, they will fight. This isn't a guess—that's what roosters do. The underground animal fighting sport known as cockfighting will happen literally every time you put two roosters next to each other. Roosters love to fight, and they will peck each other to death. Putting two roosters together may as well net you zero roosters.

Fish

If you have a pond or you want to build a pond, you can stock your own fish inside of it. These should be purchased from a decent fishery. You want to make sure that your fish are disease-free so that they won't get each other sick and die. Also, depending on the breed of fish you are going with, you need to get the male-to-female ratio right. Otherwise, you might find it overpopulating too quickly, or you might find males fighting with one another depending on the species.

Your fish can be contained within a cage inside the pond, making it very easy to scoop them out with a net—not exactly like shooting fish in a barrel but very close.

Pigs

Pigs grow fast and will eat almost anything. They consume a lot of food, around six pounds a day, and will excrete one and a half pounds of waste. Since they'll eat almost anything, they will happily eat all of your leftover foods that are in table scraps, so they never have to go to waste.

Each pig will need at least 50 square feet of space and a pen you build for them. You must keep the food and water far away from each other, optimally at opposite ends of the pen. They tend to defecate near the water. If they start contaminating their own water supply, you're going to have to change it out. It's not good for them to be eating their own waste.

Pigs are very sensitive to sunlight. You can tell because they have very little fur and very light skin. You will definitely want to give them some kind of covering. Pigs usually protect their skin by rolling around the mud, but if they don't have mud because it is a particularly dry time or dry place, then they're going to need something else.

Once a pig has stopped gaining weight, usually at around 280 pounds or more, they are ready to eat. If you know how to butcher a pig or are willing to learn, that's great. Otherwise, you ought to contact a butcher who's close to you and who can do that job for you safely and properly.

Pigs are very smart and very friendly. Not the wild ones: They will fight you. However, domesticated pigs are very friendly. There's been a growing trend where people even adopt pigs as family pets, just like dogs, and if you have not spent time around pigs, you may be surprised.

People who did not grow up on farms when they first encountered farm animals have a very different experience. People who grew up around animals and are accustomed to killing them and eating them have a very deep understanding of what meat is and where it comes from. They don't have any illusions about it. When most urban and suburban people see a chicken nugget, they don't think about it as it is.

When you spend time with a pig that you mean to ultimately slaughter and eat, it is understandable if you become emotionally attached. Your experience with animals is probable to be either pets or vermin. When the time comes, you might not feel good about killing the animal. There's no special advice on this; we're just warning you that this is a possibility. You can power through the experience and really confront what meat is, or you can decide you can't do it.

Goats

Goats are wonderful for milk and don't take up nearly as much room as cows. Some people really dislike goat milk, while others think it's really great and are willing to pay a premium for it, which is why you may see goat milk and cheese at a higher price at the store. Goats are sensitive to wind, and they need access to shade because they tend to overheat. Be sure to keep your goats and environment where they can keep cool.

Goats are natural lawn mowers. They will graze all day and keep your lawn trim. They can eat several pounds of food for a day just from grass and any hay that you supplement your diet with. They can also drink several gallons of water, more or less, depending on how much grazing they do, since a lot of their water needs are satisfied by grass.

If you are going to build them a place to live, that's a fantastic idea. They will want a place to sleep and be safe from predators and a place to keep the sun off of them—these shelters should probably be 70 square feet minimum.

There are many things in nature that will poison your goat, which they don't know better than to eat. Things like a poppy, stagger grass, and buckwheat are dangerous to a goat, so keep an eye on those.

Goats are also notorious climbers. Even domesticated goats love to climb things. A goat will even climb on top of other animals. Use an image search engine and look for yourself. Keep this in mind because if you have any way for the goat to get onto your roof, they might try to do that. If you are running solar panels on the roof, you probably don't want a goat walking around on them.

Rabbits

Rabbits are a classic option. Rabbits are perfectly fine as are any other lean game, so long as you are keeping them part of a well-balanced diet. You cannot survive on rabbit meat alone, however. There's a concept called rapid starvation, also known as protein poisoning, and it is caused by the overconsumption of protein with no fat, carbohydrates, or micronutrients.

Rabbits don't require a lot of space, which is nice. They are extremely good at escaping, though. Your rabbit cage needs to be tighter than Alcatraz; otherwise, they will get out. Rabbits are natural diggers, so you'll need to make sure that you have some caging on the ground or floor so they don't get out that particular way.

Also, rabbits are cute. If you get cold feet and do not want to butcher them, that's fine—you can always keep them as pets. However, don't let rabbit breeding get out of control, which is something that can easily happen if you aren't careful. Breeding is great if you're making food for stew, but it's not good when suddenly you have way more pets than you know what to do with. The same situation goes with pigs.

Turkey

Turkeys are an all-American bird, and you can purchase them from a turkey breeder or farm for very cheap. Turkeys are very sensitive animals, and you will likely lose several of the first few weeks after buying them. Chicks need to have a warming unit when they are, such as 100–250W lamps. They need to keep the battery at about 100 degrees Fahrenheit for the first week—they want to be toasty. After the first week, they are much less vulnerable, and you can gradually reduce the heat; after a few months, they won't need any heat at all.

Turkeys grow fast, and after three and a half months, they will be big enough that they are ready to be eaten. At 35–45 pounds, they are a lot of food, so be sure to have a way to store the meat properly or share it with others. There's a reason why a turkey is a traditional bird for Thanksgiving—many people sitting together can all share a meal together.

Turkeys are also very smelly. You do not want turkeys anywhere near your house or upwind of it. They also aren't terribly friendly. Unlike some of the other animals, they are not good pets, but they are good food.

Unlike pigs and chickens, there is no way you will get emotionally attached to a turkey. To be perfectly frank, they are mean, and their odor is very pungent. If you are squeamish about killing an animal, maybe a turkey is a good way to start because you will not feel bad.

Bees

If you have a sweet tooth, you could even consider raising bees. This is an insect that is absolutely vital to the ecosystem and great if you like sugar. Honey is the only known food that never goes bad. You need to do nothing with a container of honey to maintain it. Honey never rots. Honey will retain its edibility longer than you will be alive.

Beekeeping is a very popular hobby. It also has two wonderful side effects: It will produce honey and will pollinate your garden. The easiest way to get started with a beekeeping operation is to purchase the basic starter kits. These are not difficult to find on the Internet. A starter kit usually contains everything you need: frames, a hive feeder, a queen excluder, a smoker, and all your protective gear.

You can keep your bees within a quarter-mile of your garden, and they will do all the work of pollinating your plants. Also, where you place them can affect the flavor of the honey. Putting bees next to cloves will add a clove flavor to the honey.

It's a fun hobby and requires some research because there's more to it than you might think. Honey can also be a cool gift. Putting it in a jar and giving it to someone is a neat and personal thing.

Another by-product of raising bees is wax which can be used for sealing, protecting food to extend life, and making candles.

Dogs

No, we're not suggesting that you eat dog meat! You're not going to eat the bees either. They are just included here because we're already discussing animals.

Dog people are lucky. An off-grid lifestyle is wonderful for dogs. They have tons of space to move around, and they don't need to be taken on walks because there's nowhere for them to run off to.

Dogs also love spending time with people while working outside, which you will be doing plenty of. Dogs are essentially wolves that were genetically engineered through selective breeding to become home security systems. In a city, you'll find dogs barking at almost any noise that they hear. They bark at people walking by on the sidewalk or another dog a block away that is heading toward the sidewalk. Deep in the country, that response is essential. If you are isolated, it's unlikely that you will have unwelcome human visitors, but you can certainly expect unwelcome animal visitors. This could be foxes coming to eat your chickens, a bear simply wandering through, or a raccoon who has sniffed out your trash. Whatever it may be, dogs have extremely sharp senses of smell in hearing and will know if you have welcomed visitors long before you do, and they will eagerly tell you about it.

Foods to Grow/Stock up On

Food storage is crucial. Humans have developed many clever ways to keep their food clean and safe before refrigeration.

There are a few foods that are always good to have on hand. Even if you aren't living off-grid, having these in your home is smart.

Rice

Rice has a long shelf life, and if properly stored, rice can last six months or longer. If you also keep it refrigerated, you can get twice as much time out of it. Brown rice is an excellent source of vitamins and fiber. Brown rice is the most nutritious, and if you're eating it to stay alive, just go where the nutrition is.

Price is a staple food for more than half of the planet. That's a pretty ringing endorsement.

Beans

The best friend to rice is beans. This is a well-known and well-traveled survival food. It's also very versatile and can be used in a lot of different ways. Dried beans can be stored for a long time and can be hydrated rather quickly by soaking and heating them.

Beans are an excellent source of protein, and when complemented with rice, it forms a complete protein.

Nuts

They are an excellent source of protein and fat; dried nuts also store very well.

Cabbage

Yes, cabbage. It is low in calories but has a ton of nutrients, including B6 and C, and is very fibrous. It's also very versatile because it can be used in salads. If you are into pickling, you can turn it into sauerkraut or kimchi, a great flavor addition with a very good shelf life.

Corn

It's very easy to grow as long as the soil temperature stays high enough to allow for germination and you have mature soil. Corn is very easy to grow if you can get those two things right.

Cucumbers

If you plan on pickling, you should have cucumbers. If you are just getting cucumbers for pickling, keep in mind that there is a specific type of cucumber called a pickling cucumber. The ordinary cucumber you're used to that you put on a salad does not work the same way, but you might also like regular cucumbers.

Potatoes

Everybody loves potatoes. It's a starchy crop that's high in carbohydrates, which is important for getting your calorie intake high enough. These are crops that you are trying to live off of, and calories are your body's fuel. Yukon Gold potatoes are probably the best choice.

Sweet Potatoes

Everything we just said about potatoes is true of sweet potatoes. They are calorie dense and have much more iron nutrient content than your average potato. The leafy greens that grow on them are also edible. They have a longer growing season, longer than almost anything else you will be raising. However, sweet potatoes might be worth the extra time and effort if you like them.

Tomatoes

Setting aside the argument about whether it is a fruit or a vegetable, the tomato is a pretty easy plant as long as you give it ample water. They also like the temperature on the warm side. Tomatoes are great on so many things and can be turned into sauces, added to salads, added on top of burgers, and plenty of other applications.

Lentils

Lentils are packed with protein. It's very difficult to get a decent amount of protein from plant sources: Ask any vegetarian who is conscious of their nutrition. Lentils have around 18 grams of protein per serving—that is the same amount of protein as three eggs. Also, lentils are one of the oldest crops that humans have ever cultivated. It is ancient, and lentil soup is just delicious, so if you don't like lentils, start liking lentils.

Spinach

This plant is very easy to grow and packed with vitamins and minerals. For the adventurous, spinach can be stored by freezing it or dehydrating it and then crushing it into a powder. Now you have a powdered nutritional supplement available.

Berries

Everybody loves berries. Raspberries, cranberries, blueberries, or whatever kind of berry. They're all good. They have a lot of nutrition and a natural sweetness, and you can do a lot with them. You can turn them into jelly and incorporate them into nearly any dessert item you can think of.

Dry Seasoning and Salt

There's no reason not to make your food taste good, even in an emergency or disaster. Always have seasoning; there's no good reason not to. Dried herbs and spices last a really long time.

Dehydrating, Salting, and Smoking

For food to go bad, it needs to be wet. Salting food increases the acidity and dries it out, making bacteria grow much slower. This is exactly why beef jerky was invented. Salted meats have been with humans for as long as we've had salt.

You should consider building a smokehouse if you really enjoy food and want to go the extra mile. The process of smoking food adds a wonderful flavor that's impossible to replicate and dries out the food, which helps preserve it. Smoked salmon, for example, is delicious and a fantastic source of protein.

You can dehydrate meats, but you can also dehydrate fruits. It's also a good idea to put a type of acid on it, such as lemon juice or another citrus, because the drawing process takes a while. You want to prevent any bacteria from starting a home there during the process.

There are plenty of ways to dry food, including the inside of an oven, or you could have a special dehydrator that uses electricity. One good option is to use a non-electric dehydrator. It should take six hours minimum but can take a lot more depending on the thickness and what it is you are dehydrating in the environment. It's hard to measure exactly how much time you need to dehydrate any kind of food because, depending on your environment, it will change a lot. The outside temperature, humidity, and amount of wind passing through will greatly alter these times. With that being said, you should check in on your dehydration regularly.

Dehydrating doesn't need to use any electricity. Solar dehydrators are a great method that uses the sun to dehydrate. As long as you have a rack to place the food on, make sure that they are ventilated, they are stacked accordingly, and have netting around to keep any bugs off of it; it's not too difficult.

There are many different designs for this sort of thing—one is to create a flat box with a mesh to lay food on and then cover it with a metal covering. The sun will heat the metal, raising the internal temperature. This is a straightforward DIY method as long as there's proper ventilation underneath it to allow moisture to escape.

You can dehydrate beef and fish but DO NOT try to dehydrate birds or pigs. Exposing those kinds of animals to air for longer than is absolutely necessary is extremely dangerous. Do not do it.

Pickling and Canning

There's been a recent new interest in recreational pickling and canning. These are excellent ways to preserve food. Pickling also has the advantage of adding a vinegar flavor to whatever you want.

You can do just about anything, including meat. Things that are canned need to be adequately sealed, so double-check it. Once canned, they need to be appropriately stored in a cool place without too much sunlight. This could mean a pantry or shed. If you are in a warmer climate, you should consider digging a cellar. The sun's heat doesn't penetrate very far into the earth, and if you dig down just a short way, you can make a permanently cool space.

If a cellar is too much, it is totally fine if you want to bury your food. A hole in the ground, covered up, will be a natural refrigerator and keep the sun off and hopefully away from animals.

Cooling

Some kinds of foods absolutely need to be stored in a cool place. Some can be left at room temperature; you probably know which ones those are already. According to the FDA, certain foods will require refrigeration, and that temperature needs to be 40 degrees Fahrenheit or less. That's very close to freezing temperature. During the winter, you don't need to worry about this that much because if it is already 40 degrees and cold around, then nature is doing your refrigeration for you.

In the summer, you will need to find other ways of storing your meat, poultry, fish, dairy, certain cooked foods, eggs, and all the rest.

Certain foods you already know you can leave out are your coffee, bread, onions, honey, olive oil, and potatoes—these are all fine.

The oldest traditional method is to simply build a root cellar. A hole in the ground will be much cooler than the surface or the inside of your home during the summer.

You can always go with the old-fashioned route of getting a cooler if necessary. If you don't plan on ever storing your food for particularly long, some of the newer and more expensive coolers are extremely good at retaining cold temperature.

If you make a mistake and don't do a good job of preserving your food, look for the following symptoms: nausea, diarrhea, abdominal pain, fever, and vomiting. If you are suffering from one or more of those symptoms, especially if other people in your home are after eating the same thing, you need to reach out and contact medical help immediately—you may be suffering from food poisoning. This can be very dangerous, as it's more than just a stomachache.

Whatever food preservation method or methods you use, don't take any chances with your own health. If food looks iffy, don't take risks.

A really nice, well-insulated chest freezer and/or refrigerator are great. They use less electricity than you might expect, just as long as you don't have kids who like to hang out with the door open, looking at everything in the fridge. Don't get a cheap fridge or freezer. A really great, well-insulated fridge pays for itself.

HOW TO FEED YOURSELF WITHOUT POWER

Electric ovens crave using as much energy as possible. You cannot use an electric stove, as it is simply not realistic. Likewise, microwaves can be very power-hungry, too. They might be fine to use when you are running at peak energy intake and you have sunshine and wind, but it's not a great method. Electric stoves are terrible anyway, so nothing is lost. There are plenty more electrically conservative cooking methods that are simply better for cooking.

Wood Stove

If you already have a wood stove in your house keeping you warm, why not cook on it, too? This is an ancient and rustic way of cooking food, but it served our ancestors well for hundreds of years. The same fire that's heating up your home also has a flat surface on top. You can simply put a pot on it or a skillet and do your best to control the temperature by controlling the fire. It's not using any more power than before, so there's no reason not to utilize it.

Now it's the middle of summer, so you probably don't want to be having a piping hot fire in your living room. Try to avoid that heat as much as possible; during the summer, you will want to stay far away from any kind of fire and try one of the other options.

Solar Oven

A solar oven is a box with mirrors on the inside and a couple of missing sides. Basically, it's a big shiny device that catches solar energy and then points it into a focal point inside of it. Whatever you want to cook, you simply place it inside the container at that focal point. This will heat up whatever you are cooking on a sunny day very quickly. Think about when you touch metal on a hot day and how hot that gets.

This type of cooking is probably not great for everything. It is excellent for anything that you need to cook slowly or something that doesn't need to be cooked at a high temperature. For example, you will not be cooking steaks or kebabs on one of these things. Instead, any kind of stew would be excellent, or any kind of vegetable that you can cook slowly would be a great way to go. This is a completely green, powerless slow cooker.

There's no way to turn the temperature up or down or to regulate it in any particular way, so your best option is to check on a frequency or to place it in such a spot that after enough time, the shadow will cover it and essentially turn it off.

Propane

For cooking, you can use tanks of gas. This is just like a propane tank on a grill that you would use outside. The only difference is that it is a built-in device in your home and also contains an oven. You can't cultivate propane on your own land, which means you will need to purchase it elsewhere or have it delivered.

Gas is great for cooking and is the preferred heating element for the best chefs. It's also relatively cheap if you are just using it for cooking and not trying to heat your entire home with it.

Grilling

Just as simple as that: Everybody knows how to grill, and everybody loves grilling.

If you're using propane to grill, that's going to require you to have propane on hand. If you already happen to have propane running in your kitchen, that is very handy. If you are a charcoal kind of person, that is a great option. Charcoal doesn't go bad. You can store that for as long as you like.

Grilling means great flavor and the outdoor tradition. With a large enough surface, you can prepare a lot of food at the same time. That makes it always a great option if you have a lot of guests or a large family.

If you are raising pigs or you are doing any hunting, a pellet grill is a fantastic option for cooking large amounts of meat. Slowly add in little pellets of wood pulp—they look a lot like hamster food. This keeps feeding a fire at exactly the right amounts to maintain a steady temperature. You can get a slow cooking process going, then you wait 12 hours, culminating in an unbelievably tasty and tender meal the next day, with very little effort.

Earth Oven

Earth ovens are excellent options. You need a slab of stone, and you're going to house that using rocks and dirt to create something like a mound with a mouth on one side that food could be inserted into. Beneath, you can put in some lumber to burn. These things, once they're cooking, get ridiculously hot. If you pop an oven into this, it will be fully cooked in just a few minutes. The work on it is a very efficient way to insulate the heat, and very little gets wasted even with the open side.

When you want to keep your home as cool as possible during the summer months, cooking outside is a great way to ensure the heat stays outside. You can cook food crazy fast. From a cooking and aesthetic frame, earth ovens are just cool.

They lend themselves to cooking certain kinds of food very well, which, if you are into cooking, is a fun culinary experiment. Also, they happen to be very easy to build. They're all so very cheap because mostly what you need are brick and dirt. Anyone can make one with a few simple instructions.

LIVING OFF THE LAND

Depending on your environment and your personal ethics, you can do what people have done for millennia. Nature readily provides protein in the form of animals. Hunting is undoubtedly an option that you can avail yourself of if you want.

This isn't a book about hunting, and we won't go into deep detail about it, but if it is something you're interested in, there are plenty of resources available so that you can learn more about the topic.

States and counties have many hunting, fishing, and trapping laws, and you will need to learn them to not break any laws.

Don't Eat Wild Mushrooms

This should go without saying, but some people don't know: Do NOT eat wild mushrooms. We cannot say this strongly enough. We don't care if you have a book on identifying mushrooms. Unless you are a mycologist, do not go putting wild mushrooms in your mouth. Mushrooms can be very dangerous. Even with photographs, the differences between a safe one and a dangerous one can be indistinguishable.

Also, don't eat berries. Don't eat things in the woods if you don't know what you're doing.

Hunting

There are considerations about what kinds of animals you can hunt during which portion of the season. Hunting with a gun usually has a very short season. An average size buck can net you an average of 60 or 70 pounds of meat. A boar can net you double that, which is a lot of meat. You should have some friends or a good way to store it.

If you're using more difficult means of hunting, such as a bow or a black powder rifle, you will have a larger season to hunt in.

If you live in a remote area that has dangerous wildlife such as bears or cougars, having a form of self-defense might be very valuable. Bear spray and other nonlethal weapons are good to have, but if your concern is protecting yourself from a mama bear who feels threatened by you, you're going to want the best tool that you can avail yourself of. This can mean a 10mm pistol at your side, or a strong hunting rifle chambered in something like 6.5mm Creedmoor.

Most animals are not interested in you and will not pick a fight with you. However, starving and desperate animals might take their chances; an animal that perceives you as a threat to their young might attack you. These kinds of attacks don't happen often, but when they do, they are brutal. People are torn apart, isolated in the wilderness, and unable to contact medical aid easily.

A well-placed shot will kill an animal so quickly that they are dead before they realize what has happened. Taking a bad shot and wounding an animal is a serious faux pas among hunters. Hunters do not want to hurt animals: They want to hunt animals. Wounding an animal is cruel, and tracking a wounded animal to finish the job is not anyone's idea of fun.

If you are interested in hunting but are not experienced, your best bet is to make friends with someone who is. There are a lot of things to learn, not just the laws, of which any good hunter will be well aware. There are many things you should familiarize yourself with before you go walking around in the woods with a gun and no idea what you are doing. There are also considerations, like how to safely harvest what you need, how to kill an animal most humanely, how to stay downwind of an animal, or how to transport it after being shot.

Fishing

Fishing is a great form of recreation, and the catch you get will be a great form of protein. If you have access to water that has edible fish, that can be a great asset. Depending on where you live, you might have fishing options all over. You aren't locked to your property, remember. There may be great lakes and streams close enough that you can walk or drive and get yourself a meal—with a fishing license, naturally.

For the truly committed fish eater, you can build an artificial pond and populate it with your own supply of fish. With a river, you can trap fish with zero effort and come by and pick them up as you like.

Trapping

Trapping is a tricky business but has been a staple for eons. Trapping doesn't mean those terrifying spiky metal claws, like bear traps. Those are illegal, so do not use them. If you have one, we don't know where you found one, but don't use it.

Trapping usually means cages and snares. Once again, this depends on your local law, and you need to investigate it before you get involved. The advantage of trapping is that you don't need to do anything other than set up the traps and visit them occasionally. This generates a passive supply of animals without the work of chasing.

It's simply pieces of twine that are attached in certain strategic locations.

If you are tracking, you may be able to find common routes for rabbits. If they find a path they like, they will keep using it, knowing it is a relatively safe trail. However, if you know about it, it is not so safe for them. A live trap or a snare in one of these spots could nab you a bunny.

If you are the kind of person that isn't squeamish about eating squirrels, just know that they are very easy to catch in a snare. Simply by taking a piece of wood and leaning against a tree, squirrels are lazy like all animals and take the path of least resistance. Squirrels always walk up the branch leaning against the tree, which makes a branch the perfect place to leave a snare.

Snaring and trapping is a game of numbers. The more traps you have set out, the more likely you are to catch any animal. Whatever traps you have on your property, you should check them a couple of times a day just to see if anything is there.

Snare traps are cheap, but live traps are easy. Just simply get a cage that will close itself when something goes inside of it. Bait that with something the animal of your preference likes and visit to see if anyone took the bait.

KEY CHAPTER TAKEAWAYS

- **Lesson #1: Growing Your Own Food**

Because you will be practicing self-sufficiency living off-grid, you will also need to grow your own food. Through gardening, you will be able to produce fruits, vegetables, herbs, and more.

- **Lesson #2: Raising Livestock For Self-Sufficiency**

If meat is a big part of your diet, you should consider raising your own farm animals. The easiest animals to raise would be chickens, fish, pigs, goats, rabbits, turkeys, and even bees.

- **Lesson #3: The Best Food to Grow & Stock up on**

In case of emergencies, it's good to have food with long shelf-lives which you can store and eat in case you run out of your other food. Some in this list are the easiest vegetables to grow, which will also help your strength and health.

- **Lesson #4: Eating Even Without Power**

Since there might be some minor setbacks sometimes, you might not be able to cook your food in the usual way. Even without electricity, some options to eat are using a wood stove, solar oven, propane, grilling, and earth oven.

- **Lesson #5: Other Ways to Eat Off-Grid**

Some other ways to have a source of nutrition are foraging, hunting, fishing, and trapping. You must also consider the laws in your area for these practices.

BECOME SELF-SUFFICIENT EASIER THAN EVER

While not everyone has a natural green thumb or a connection to animals like Dr. Doolittle, you can still discover ways to make it work for you. You don't need the talent to supply yourself with food once you live off-grid, but you certainly need to know what you're doing.

If you book a call with us today, you'll find that things that left you feeling more clueless and confused than when you started are things of the past. You'll be supplied with ample knowledge from experts who can guide you along the way.

OFF GRID NUTRITION AND HOMESTEADING CHECK-IN EXERCISE

Before we proceed with the rest of the book, let's first explore where you are right now in your Off Grid Journey.

Below, rate yourself on a scale of one to five on how accurate the statements are for you — a score of one means "not accurate," and a score of five means "very accurate."

After you have rated yourself according to the statements, add the sum total of your scores, then read "What Your Score Really Means" to determine the outcome of your results.

Check-in Statement	Rating

I have begun growing my own food in my garden.	
I have knowledge of how to grow my own food.	
I know the easiest vegetables to plant to get started.	
I know the vegetables with the shortest harvest cycles.	
I know the best foods to stock up on with the longest shelf life.	
I know the different ways to store and preserve my food.	
I know how to cook food in case there is no power.	
I have begun researching how to raise different livestock.	
I have decided to raise livestock.	
I know how to forage and do it often.	
TOTAL SCORE:	

WHAT YOUR SCORE REALLY MEANS

Score: 0 - 15

Feed Yourself With More Knowledge

It's time to get serious about your off-grid venture so you can both take care of yourself and your family. Making sure you and your family are well fed with the most amazing meals will make your home all the more enjoyable. All you have to do is to know more about gardening. Even if you're not planning to be completely self-sufficient by raising livestock, it would still do you good to have more knowledge on it.

Score: 16 - 30

Take Your Skills to the Next Level

Now that you have the knowledge to take care of yourself off-grid, you must start planning your practice. Even if you're not yet living off-grid, you can start small by planting vegetables in your backyard or even in pots in your apartment. If you put in the effort, it's possible to really get started even before the big move.

Score: 31+

Grow Your Self-Sufficient Garden

You are now at a point where you probably have sufficient knowledge on growing your own food and even raising livestock. Now it's time to improve your skills by planting even more.

Begin planting vegetables, fruits, herbs, and even trees! If you have decided on raising your own farm animals, you can start small with chickens by taking care of them, cleaning their coop daily, and having the benefits of fresh eggs. Remember, your knowledge won't be of any use until you actually put in the work.

CHAPTER 6: HEATING AND COOLING YOUR OFF-GRID HOME

Chapter six gives a spiel on the different possible choices for heating and cooling systems in your off-grid home, including the pros and cons of each, how they work, and how they can be installed.

Outside where the cold, harsh winds come, or the scorching heat arises, we tend to retreat to our homes where warmth can envelop us or cool air from fans can soothe us. But when you live off-grid, things can get a whole lot sticker and chillier if you don't plan it well.

We need a suitable place to stay safe and warm when winter comes. The climate can hurt our health if we're cold for too long. Some of the effects are worsening asthma attacks, arthritis, depression, and more ailments.

If you're able to plan and set up a sustainable heating system, your home can be a haven from the biting cold, where you can curl up with mugs of hot chocolate with your family.

As for the summer, you not only have to worry about cooling yourself but also your animals if you choose to raise livestock. When the heat is too much, our health can also be affected. Fevers, migraines, and even something as serious as a stroke can happen!

It's crucial that you find ways to stay cool in your off-grid home because you'll also have to do tasks outside your home. A cool breeze with a nice cold drink will help you against the heat waves!

From this chapter, you'll learn how you can stay toasty warm throughout the cold weather and refreshingly cool throughout summer days. Living off-grid and comfortably living don't have to be separate things. If you know what to do, your journey will be a pleasant and cozy time!

Geothermal energy has existed for billions of years, but archaeological evidence shows that the first human use of geothermal resources began around 10,000 years ago. In North America, Paleo-Indians encountered hot springs. Because of the heat and comfort they brought, they decided to settle there. They then used the hot springs as a source of warmth, bathing, and healing.

Further down the line, geothermal energy was put into industrial use in 1892 in Boise, Idaho. The residents here experienced the first-ever district heating system in the world. The heat from the hot springs was extracted as the water was piped from them to the town. This amazing heating system provided hundreds of homes with warmth, and to this day, this invention still makes its rounds.

It's known that geothermal heating is one of the best sustainable choices for those wanting to live off-grid. Now, looking back to the past and seeing the people who first used geothermal energy, we can see how significant it still is today because it can still serve its purpose incredibly in this modern age.

Heating and cooling are easy to leave as afterthoughts until the moment you need them. You will be miserable if the temperature gets too hot or too cold. If it gets bad enough, it can be lethal. There are a lot of options here, which is nice.

To be perfectly honest, if a lot of things aren't going great, you can put up with it. If you have to haul your water out or if you can't get your garden running and have to go to the grocery store, you can still live with it. However, if you live in a home that is 95 degrees Fahrenheit for a week, you will most likely abandon this project as soon as possible. No one can be expected to live like that when there is a cozy Holiday Inn just 25 miles away.

If your temperature is off, everything else will be off, too, so this is one thing you definitely need to get right.

If you have animals, don't forget them! If you are hot, they are hot; if you are cold, they are cold.

HEATING AND COOLING

What's better than having a heating system and a cooling system? Having a system that both helps heating and cooling at the same time. These are integral to the house and are both fantastic systems. Geothermal and passive solar designs are great for all kinds of temperature regulation, both hot and cold. They should be integrated into the home when it's built. Retrofitting a house after the fact might cost you more money and trouble than it's worth.

Geothermal

We already discussed geothermal energy in a previous chapter, so we don't want to repeat too much of what was there. Geothermal is outstanding for temperature control because it draws on air that is always cooler than outside when it is hot and always warmer than when it is freezing outside.

Geothermal works by running a winding series of pipes underground, then they draw water through those pipes with a pump that will enter your home. Sometimes, these pipes will run through the floor and the walls.

The upfront costs can be high, but it is one of the most energy-efficient options for comfortably keeping the temperature out of your home.

After you dig ten feet under the ground, it's always 55 degrees Fahrenheit, no matter what time of year it is. If it's 100 degrees out, ten feet down is 55 degrees. It gets to be minus ten outside, ten feet down; it's still 55 degrees.

A geothermal heating system runs water at this temperature. It is then able to transmit it to the air using water pumps and fans. This uses some electricity but much less than a standard heating or cooling system.

Depending on the space, this can cost several thousands to build, so it will also save a lot of money if you put it together yourself. This isn't too difficult but does require a lot of work.

Geothermal is a very cool system, and there isn't any home that wouldn't benefit from a geothermal system.

Passive Solar Design

Passive solar design is clever architecture and a design of the building itself to maximize heat when you need it and minimize heat when you want it to be cooler.

There's a very important mosque in Israel called the Dome of the Rock. It is considered very important and has a very clever design. The mosque is a large stone dome. When the sun rises, it begins to heat the rock, but it takes a while for this heat to penetrate the stone and reach the inside. By the time it begins to heat the mosque, enough time has passed that the sun is already beginning its descent on the Western horizon. Then, throughout the night, the stone that was used throughout the day cools, and by the morning, the schedule repeats itself. By simply having a dome of exactly the right amount of stone, it can keep the occupants of the mosque comfortable even in the tremendous scorching summers of the Middle East.

Passing solar design in a modern house uses techniques like this. By choosing exactly where the windows are, facing them toward the sunlight at particular times of day can make an enormous impact. Choosing where to place awnings so that the sunlight will not get in through windows, depending on where it is in the sky, also has a significant impact. The particular place you choose to keep a wood-burning stove or trees around the property in the home and how that blocks out sunlight is also a considerable factor.

Any kind of passive solar design will be wholly integrated with the house. We need to factor in things like the direction in which the wind blows. It needs to take into consideration the trees and hills nearby. A good passive solar design will be completely customized for that particular environment, so two houses with passive solar designs will often look very different depending on where they are.

For that reason, passive solar design is a little bit like feng shui. You most likely won't know how to do it, and if it's something that interests you, you are going to need to learn a heck of a lot of things before you attempt it yourself. Alternatively, you can reach out and look for architects or contractors who are familiar with passive solar design, and you can help you come up with something that you are happy with.

For the sake of this book, we can't go into too much depth about solar design because that could be an entire book in itself. However, you are encouraged to look into it if you design your own home. You can get a lot of interesting ideas that cost you next to nothing but will make your heating and cooling considerably cheaper.

HEATING YOUR HOME

Wood Stove

The most popular way to eat in your home would be with the classic stove fireplace. These are just lovely to look at, and seeing fire gives off a cozy atmosphere. Many of these can also be used as a stovetop where pots can be placed directly on top to cook with. These things get extremely hot, so this might not be a good option if you have small children.

To operate these things, you also need to clean them regularly, and you will need to get firewood. Firewood can be found, purchased, made, and would need to be kept dry. Wood also needs to be prepared, so large logs should be split into halves, quarters, and smaller pieces.

You'll need a chimney, and if you have small children, you will absolutely need a barrier of some kind to keep your kids away. These things get HOT, and no one wants to see a toddler get a bad burn by touching one of these.

Wood stoves give really warm energy, and we don't just mean heat. They have a certain vibe that they give to a room. They come in all varieties, some very traditional and some very modern.

You'll need firewood way ahead of actually needing wood. That means you need your wood chopped, dry, and in large supply well ahead of when you plan on burning it. Green, freshly cut wood doesn't burn well and kicks out sparks. Put your wood someplace dry. Building a barrier over a woodpile to keep the rain off is basically mandatory. Also, you should have your logs already chopped into quarters and smaller bits. The small pieces will be needed as kindling to get the fire going, and once it's cooking, you'll want to be feeding this fire with quarter logs or at least halves. If you are chilling on a cold, winter night, you don't want to have to make a trip outside to chop wood.

Two major drawbacks of the woodfire stove are that they need to be cleaned regularly. You're going to have to get in there with a shovel and remove all of the ash. It's inside your house, so you have to be careful not to get gray dust onto everything. Ashes are a good source of compost, so be sure to add them to anything you want to use to grow.

The other drawback of the woodfire stove is, of course, fire safety. If you aren't careful about managing the fire to a good level and it gets too big, or if there's some kind of congestion in the chimney, you may find your house filling with smoke or starting a fire. Whether you have a woodfire stove or not, you should own a fire extinguisher. You are probably living far away from any fire department. Everyone needs a fire extinguisher, and that's doubly true if you are building fires inside your home.

Compost Water Heater

Compost heating sounds pretty gross, but if you do it right, don't worry: It won't be gross at all. As organic material breaks down, part of the process is that as microorganisms break down the material, their life cycle releases heat. Compost heating captures this heat and moves it into a conductive source such as water, and then, you can use that water as it is almost warm, or you can pump it through a system to heat up your home.

A compost pile of wood chips can actually put out a considerable amount of heat. You'll notice it because usually these things are left outdoors, and the heat dissipates immediately. A good compost heap gets hotter than you might think.

Running pipes through a compost heats the same way that you would for geothermal, achieving a similar effect. The heat is transferred into the pipe water. The heat is there. All you have to do is capture it. You can also use this water to heat a greenhouse if you are using one or through a radiant heat floor system. You can even find instances of people using it to heat up a hot tub all year. In the last chapter of this book, we'll go into greater detail about how to compost, but for now, it's sufficient to mention that a compost pile will get very hot, up to 150 degrees Fahrenheit. That is much hotter than most people would feel comfortable relaxing in.

Radiant Heat Floor

Try radiant floor heating if you can heat up a lot of water using composting or solar energy. Radiant floor heating looks a lot like compost heating and geothermal but in reverse. The way it works is that hot water is run in piping that zigzags underneath the floor. The pipes touch aluminum plating, which is attached to wood. Simply having the pipes making contact with the metal and wood transmits the heat, and a small amount of heat generates upward from the floor. Since heat rises, it creates a general, warm and ambient temperature. Also, because it's just spread out, no fans are necessary. The heat doesn't just turn on and off based on what a thermometer reads.

A system like this requires a lot of piping and specially made floors. They also need a reliable pump system to keep the water moving.

People spend good money to enjoy heated flooring systems in their bathrooms. These have become very popular with those that can afford them. The radiant floor heating works on the same principle but is much cooler than the bathroom heating. They just heat one room, but you can heat your whole house. Incidentally, if you have a pet cat, they will love this.

Cooling Your Home

It's easier to warm up than it is to cool off. Keeping cool is a very tricky business that has been with humans for the entire history of our species. Our ancestors had to find solutions with much fewer resources and technology than we have now.

One of the considerations for where you choose to live will certainly involve your heat tolerance. Some people feel comfortable in warm environments, and other people just sweat, melt, and feel miserable. You're going to be feeling pretty miserable if you move out to your new home and are deteriorating in 90-degree weather all summer long. Managing your heat is super important.

Thankfully, some options are relatively power efficient and won't require a lot of electricity.

Air Conditioning

One of the greatest modern inventions ever made is the air conditioner. We tend to think of it as a luxury good, but it has profoundly impacted human life.

Water is extremely conductive. That means electricity passes through it easily, and it collects heat easily. Imagine if you put a pot of water in the oven and set the temperature to 500 degrees Fahrenheit, letting it sit for a couple of hours. If you were to reach your hand into the oven, you would feel the heat in your hand, but it wouldn't burn you immediately. If you put your hand in the bucket, you would cook your hand. The water is very conductive, but the air isn't.

The way your body manages heat is by sweating. Since water is conductive, and saltwater is extra conductive, the heat stays in the sweat as it leaves the body. The sweat falls off or dries away, carrying the heat with it. In principle, air conditioning works the same way, using a compressor and an expansion valve filled with refrigerant fluid.

You've seen your electric bills in the summer, so you already know that air conditioners are costly to keep running—these are electrically hungry machines.

That said, if the sun is shining and heating you up, they are also feeding your solar systems if you have one. This means that air conditioners are a ripe instance where you can take advantage of opportunity usage, which we covered earlier in the chapter about generating power. If you have enough solar power feeding your air conditioner, the sheets that are making you boil are the exact same energy that is going to cool you down.

Solar Chimney

Solar chimneys work on a very clever principle. You run a black pipe through the roof just like any other chimney, tap it off so that rainfall won't come in it, and put a grate in it so that animals won't climb down it. Since the pipe is black, it will absorb more solar energy and heat it up. Likewise, the air inside of the pipe will also heat up. Hot air rises. When the air in the pipe begins to rise up, it creates a suction effect that pulls air up out of the house itself.

On another portion, or portions of the house, there is also great air intake. Since the hot air at the chimney is creating a suction effect and pulling air through the house, the new air will come in through the cold vents, or the geothermal system does add cool air into the home. There's always somewhere that is relatively cool—this could be in the shade or from your geothermal system.

These systems are very different from your traditional methods. Some people have great success with these, and others don't. It's certainly something that requires thought and planning to maximize its benefits.

The major drawback of this design is that you cannot retrofit a building—it has to be designed as an integral part of the architecture.

Solar Fans

You can't go wrong with fans. Fans are cheap and don't require a lot of power. In fact, when you need to fan the most, the sun is usually shining. Solar fans are often an excellent option. Fans inside of an animal's space will help keep them cool and also help ventilate any smells. Solar fans are also recommended to be placed inside any greenhouse you build. This will help regulate the temperature inside. Plants like it hot, but they don't like it too hot.

If you're clever about it, you can find cool spaces near your house, using a fan to blow the cool air in and a different fan to push the hot air out. You can run a pipe or something through a shady area for your intake fan. You can also run an output fan at a higher level where the hottest air goes.

This is a very low-tech solution. We would not recommend using this alone. This is a good way to supplement any other cooling system that you have, but it probably won't be sufficient on its own, just like rainwater is insufficient to cover all of your water needs.

Sun Oven and Outdoor Fires

You do not want to cook food indoors on a hot day. All the heat produced will just make your home that much hotter. Cooking outside is a great solution. It's no accident that summer is the grilling season.

Sun Oven is the perfect product to reduce indoor heat. It's a box with a couple of open sides and reflective surfaces inside. This works exactly as you would expect. The sun reflects and cooks whatever you place inside the Sun Oven. It's not fast—it works like a slow cooker, which makes it great for stews and chili.

KEY CHAPTER TAKEAWAYS

- **Lesson #1: The Different Ways to Heat & Cool Your Home**

Some systems allow for both the heating and cooling of your home. Some of these are geothermal power and having a passive solar design for your home.

- **Lesson #2: Heating Systems For Your Off Grid Home**

Some ways to heat your home off-grid are by using a wood stove, compost water heater, and radiant heat floor.

- **Lesson #3: Cooling Systems For Your Off-Grid Home**

This lesson introduces some energy-efficient ways to cool your home. These would be air conditioning, solar chimney, solar fans and sun ovens, and outdoor fires.

Learn Proven Strategies for an Independent Lifestyle

You won't always have the time to devote to your venture into an off-grid life. We understand that wholeheartedly, and that's why we created this guide and even more insider lessons to make things much easier for you.

Researching, learning, and understanding all of these take a lot of time, but with us, you'll be able to cut that time to nearly half or more! So book a call with us today and see the possibilities for yourself.

OFF GRID TEMPERATURE SYSTEMS CHECK-IN EXERCISE

Before we proceed with the rest of the book, let's first explore where you are right now in your Off Grid Journey.

Below, rate yourself on a scale of one to five on how accurate the statements are for you -- a score of one means "not accurate," and a score of five means "very accurate."

After you have rated yourself according to the statements, add the sum total of your scores, then read "What Your Score Really Means" to determine the outcome of your results.

Check-in Statement	Rating
I know the different ways to heat and cool my off-grid home.	
I have begun researching off-grid heating systems.	
I have chosen an off-grid heating system.	
I have a set budget for my off-grid heating system.	
I have set up my heating system.	

I have begun researching off-grid cooling systems.	
I have chosen an off-grid cooling system.	
I have a set budget for my off-grid cooling system.	
I have set up my off-grid cooling system.	
I know the advantages and disadvantages of each system.	
TOTAL SCORE:	

WHAT YOUR SCORE REALLY MEANS

Score: 0 - 15

Warm Your Mind Up With Learning

Comfort and living off-grid, as you probably already know, don't have to be separate things. It's also important for your health to keep the temperatures at bay. That's why it's time to review and take things seriously, for you, your family, and even your livestock, if you choose to raise any!

Score: 16 - 30

Assess Your Needs and Decide

After gathering all of your information, you need to make a final decision. Approach the subject by carefully dissecting your needs and what is most feasible for you. Lay out all the pros and cons, and soon enough, you'll find the best choice for everyone. Setting up a budget plan can also make things much clearer as well.

Your next big goal now is to answer: What do I need to have my ideal systems set up? Make sure to write everything down to make things infinitely easier. Take note whether the system you've chosen will need extra help in building it. Creating a realistic timeline for how things will flow can also set your expectations straight.

CHAPTER 7: OFF-GRID WASTE MANAGEMENT

In Chapter seven, you'll learn how to handle waste in your off-grid home, along with waste systems that you can choose from and a detailed description of each option.

One TEDx speaker, Lauren Singer, prefaced their presentation by proudly showing a 16-oz jar that fits all the trash they had produced over the past three years.

In their presentation, not only did they identify the causes but also provided resolutions to waste management.

According to Singer, there are three main sources of waste:

1. Food packaging

   - Resolution: Try to shop in bulk

2. Product packaging

   - Resolution: Learn how to *make* all products you need

3. Organic food waste

   - Resolution: Learn how to compost

From the resolutions stated arise the benefits: things become cheaper because you learn to make things on your own. You eat better because you don't buy processed food products anymore. You feel better because you're healthier. Simply put: when you eat better, feel better, and save better, you become happier.

Singer has inspired thousands of people to produce less to zero waste by being mindful of what they buy, what they make, how they manage their waste and being sustainable. The jar is proof that if they can make it possible, what's stopping you from doing the same?

"I want to be remembered for the things that I did while I was on this planet, and not for the trash that I left behind." (Singer, 2015)

Nobody really wants to deal with trash and waste. The awful stench and the bacteria are enough to make us recoil from nausea. And in the city, it's pretty much maintained for you, but once you live off-grid, this will also be one of your responsibilities to keep.

First, you'll need to think about your trash. Where will you discard that waste? There are laws in place on how to keep things sanitary, so you'll need to keep that in mind as well.

Second, you need to take into account your water waste as well; this is the water you use after bathing, washing your hands, or cleaning pretty much anything. This is called *gray*

water, and you'll need to decide on a good way to deal with it.

For you to live off-grid, you need to keep things as sanitary as possible to stay healthy and keep your home safe. Furthermore, your waste in the bathroom also needs to be managed. You need to learn about systems to put in place, and throughout this

chapter, you'll discover the best one for you.

Waste management is vital and also one of the things we think about least when considering living off the grid. When you live on a plumbing and sewage system and have regular garbage collection, you don't have to think about this much. However, when waste disposal becomes your job to take care of, you will understand how important it really is.

DO NOT dump your septic waste on your property. It is gross, illegal, and dangerous. Even if animals use the wilderness as their restroom, you should not be doing the same.

TRASH AND COMPOSTING

Any leftover material that you throw out, such as dinner scraps, leftover food that has gone bad, or little bits of meat on the bones of ribs you cooked the night before, can be used to fuel your garden.

There's no need to waste perfectly good material. Even things like coffee grounds, eggshells, and ash can be great in a garden. You will definitely want to have a separate place to dispose of compostable materials and set that aside. If you own pigs, they are always happy to have any scraps or leftovers that you are done with.

If you're doing any gardening, and you probably are, you will definitely want a compost pile.

There are two kinds of composting: hot and cold. Cold is as simple as taking the waste and putting it in a container or pile and letting them decompose.

Hot composting requires more work, but it speeds up the process. When the weather is warm, you can speed it up so that it is done in a month or two. To get faster composting, you will need oxygen, water, carbon, and nitrogen. All these things will help feed the microorganisms that will consume the matter, speeding up the rate of decay.

You can also speed this up by purchasing worms. Specifically, you need red worms, also sometimes called red wigglers. These are not hard to find. You won't use the nightcrawlers you buy for fishing or any other worm. Any place with a decent gardening supply section should be able to help you out.

Whatever the bio trash you are using, you are also going to want to add nitrogen-rich material. This would include grass trimmings, leaves, tree branches, newspaper, hay, cardboard, and wood chips. Any of these materials should be mixed in with your composting material.

If you aren't getting much rain, you'll need to water the pile regularly, just like it's a garden of trash. You're not trying to get totally soaked—you just want to add enough water so that the microorganisms can do their job. However, don't add so much that you drown your red wigglers. If you can put your hand inside of it and feel it's producing a lot of heat, you are doing it right.

About every week or so, you should turn your pile over and let it mix. To do this with the shovel or pitchfork, just keep it moving. Make sure it's getting oxygen in the center. At this point, it should be getting very hot, up to 150 degrees.

Your compost is done when it stops putting out lots of heat. It should start looking like dirt again. At that point, it is perfect for your garden, so go ahead and transplant that dirt and all your red wigglers into their new home.

Trash

Anything that isn't compostable, biodegradable, or burnable, such as plastic, should be placed in a container and set aside. Since you don't have a trash removal service coming to your location, you will need to take it to a dump yourself or arrange for someone to come and get it. Hopefully, the amount of this kind of waste will diminish over time, and these trips will become less frequent.

Burn

Some things are perfectly fine to burn, such as wood or cotton, cloth, paper towel rolls, and dryer lint. Again, just like the water, don't set anything on fire that will create toxicity. Don't try burning plastic or metal with paint on it or something else you wouldn't want to breathe.

When burning things, always do so responsibly. Don't start a fire if you live in a dry climate during a dry spell. Starting fires can be very risky in certain places like Wyoming and Colorado. If you are going to use a burn barrel, just be careful, and be sure to have a fire extinguisher close by.

We're sure we sound like a broken record, but here it is: Make sure it is legal to burn your trash. Different places have different rules. If you're deep enough back from the road, probably no one will see you, but it needs to be said.

GRAY WATER

Gray water is dirty water from your sink or shower—this isn't toilet water. It's simple enough to get rid of so long as you aren't using soaps and detergents with harmful chemicals. If you are using all-natural stuff to wash your body and your dishes, then this water can simply be grounded out of the house and dropped onto the soil working to be reabsorbed by the earth. Be sure that nothing you deposit is going to be harmful and harm the plants or wildlife out there or be something that you don't want anything to do with the groundwater.

Make sure nothing that goes into the gray water is harmful. You can check all your labels and investigate if you have any doubts. If you are using harmful detergents and soaps, you can always put those into a septic system.

Depending on how you set up your water, there are many ways to capture and separate your gray water from your septic system. It can be simply diverted into a bucket. As simple as that sounds, that's completely viable. Gray water could also be diverted toward a particular use that you have in mind. For example, gray water, provided that it is clean enough that it won't hurt plants, could potentially be diverted into the yard to be reabsorbed by the soil. If you are especially confident of the quality of your gray water, you could even divert it to your garden to water plants.

Gray water that is dirty can also be used to flush toilets, wash your clothes, or wash your car. That is a good way to get multiple uses out of one batch of water and get much more efficient use for it. That's definitely more preferable than dumping it in a septic system.

SEPTIC SYSTEM

Probably the most popular option is to install a septic system. A septic system is a gigantic tank buried underground just like a water tank, but instead of holding water, it holds everything you flush down the toilet. If you have any kind of internal plumbing in your home, you are definitely going to need this. We don't want the septic system boiling, and we don't want it freezing. Both will be a worse disaster than bursting the water tanks.

Tanks have a hatch, and you will need to periodically have a waste removal truck come and suck out the waste that is stored there. Depending on the size of your tank and how many people live in your home, this could be only once every few years.

OUTHOUSE

It may not be surprising to know that most people don't want to use an outhouse. Outhouses are a very old way of doing things. They don't require any water and are very easy to build. To use the bathroom, you'll have to leave your house, and if it's in the dead of winter, that's not too fun.

If you don't want to live a life within our house, they might be useful as a start-up way to have a restroom until you are completely building a more permanent one. If your properties are particularly large, you might find that putting in an outhouse at the far end will be helpful when walking around so that you don't have to hike all the way back to your home for number two.

COMPOSTING TOILET

This isn't very attractive for everyone, but it's actually really great. A composting toilet does not use water. If you remember from the earlier chapter on setting up your water, toilet flushes account for a huge amount of the water that you go through.

Composting toilets can be purchased or built from scratch. You won't need a septic system so long as you have a suitable means of disposing of your gray water.

Essentially, this is a system to dump in a bucket and turn your own waste into human compost. Yes, that sounds pretty gross, but it's not as bad as you think. You save a lot of water, and it's very eco-friendly.

Your waste is caught in a bucket with sawdust. The sawdust works a lot like cat litter; it absorbs your waste and also cuts down on the smell. The drier, the better. Some have two separate chambers: one for urine and one for feces.

In your home, you're going to want a fan system to ventilate odors out of your home. Some water mixed with vinegar in a spray bottle can also help a lot.

When you've got a full bucket, haul it out to your composting heap. This is by far the greenest option of all of them. If you are particularly concerned about conservation, this is your best bet.

One way to know who your real friends are is to invite them for a soak in a hot tub hooked up to a compost heat system, heated using your own human manure.

KEY CHAPTER TAKEAWAYS

- **Lesson #1: Composting & Dealing With Trash Off-Grid**

Disposing of your trash will depend solely on you. You must learn how to compost and properly throw out the correct trash.

- **Lesson #2: Disposing of Gray Water**

Gray water is used water from your sink or shower. Some people also re-use it for other purposes if the water isn't harmful. You will need to choose a way to collect and dispose of it.

- **Lesson #3: The Different Systems For Waste Management**

The different types of waste systems are a septic system, outhouse, and composting toilet. The prices of each vary, and some will require a professional team to handle them.

The Breakthrough You're Waiting For

Many times, we're really just waiting for that big break for ourselves, aren't we? We're waiting to win that lottery ticket, get that promotion, or even just for normal life to come again.

But the thing is, waiting without action won't do anything to change our lives. So today, we're urging you to take hold of your life once again. Your breakthrough is near and possible if you do something about it.

We created this guide to help you jumpstart your journey, but if you want to take it even further, we're here to help. Hop on a call with us, and your success will be just within reach.

OFF GRID WASTE MANAGEMENT CHECK-IN EXERCISE

Before we proceed with the rest of the book, let's first explore where you are right now in your Off Grid Journey.

Below, rate yourself on a scale of one to five on how accurate the statements are for you -- a score of one means "not accurate," and a score of five means "very accurate."

After you have rated yourself according to the statements, add the sum total of your scores, then read "What Your Score Really Means" to determine the outcome of your results.

Check-in Statement	Rating
I no longer depend on waste systems in the city.	
I know how to compost.	
I know how to dispose of gray water.	
I know the different kinds of off-grid waste management systems.	
I have researched the different options for waste management.	
I have chosen a waste management system for my off-grid home.	

I know the advantages and disadvantages of waste systems.	
I have a set budget for my chosen waste management system.	
I know how to dispose of trash in my off-grid home.	
TOTAL SCORE:	

WHAT YOUR SCORE REALLY MEANS

Score: 0 - 15   **Declutter Your Mind**

Right now, you must be seeing how there's so much needed to fix to live off-grid. And you're right; it's no piece of cake. There are a lot of responsibilities that go into it, even your waste management!

And so, supplying yourself with enough knowledge is essential, but taking a breather, stepping back, and looking at the bigger picture can help you even more. Clear your head and set your goal in place.

Score: 16 - 30   **Organize Your Options**

You are doing a great job in taking in enough knowledge on the subject, but you still need to take a few steps ahead. Now that you know more, it's time to organize the variety of options set before you. List down all the pros and cons, your set budget, and those you like the most in general. Carefully considering all the factors will help you make a final decision.

Score: 31+   **Take Action**

Once you've chosen your ideal wastage system and you know exactly how it'll function in your home, you are now ready to set things up yourself. If you can take it on your own, purchase all the materials, resources, and items you need to begin. If you need extra help to get things done, research and contact the right people for the job. Keep reviewing how things will be set up and create another timeline for this process. You will now be well on your way to completing your off-grid journey and finally enjoying it for yourself.

An Outline to Start Your New Home

This is the order of operations to get your homestead off the ground. You can use this as a general outline or a worksheet, a place to get your mind moving and to get the process of planning moving.

Step One: Make a Decision

This is the biggest step of all. Simply choose if you want to do it. You will need to consider if this is good for your family overall. Make sure that everyone involved understands and is happy to participate. If you have a spouse and children, they need to be okay with all this stuff, too.

Step Two: Planning

The more planning you do, the easier and smoother all the rest of the steps are.

- Figure out your budget.
- Research locations.
- Choose a state and county.
- If you are moving far away, you will have to figure out work if you can't do it remotely—that might mean looking for a new job.
- Calculate your power consumption; estimate how much power you can generate.
- Calculate your water consumption; estimate how much water you can produce.

You want to have an estimate of all the material costs. There's the price of land and if you live in a state with property taxes. If there's going to be an interruption to your income, that's going to have to be figured out.

You also want a buffer room. It is a sure thing that things will go wrong. That's not an off-grid thing; that's a life thing. You might make an error, wire your electrical system incorrectly, and accidentally torch your inverter. You might have horrendous weather that slows you down. Maybe a clever fox finds their way into your chicken coop. Things always go wrong, and they take time, energy, and money to make them right.

STEP THREE: FIND LAND

Once all the other considerations have been weighed, and you know what you are looking for, go find it and buy it. The two most important things are:

- A place where you are actually allowed to live off-grid without too much interference from red tape and regulation.
- A source of water.

If you are going to need a deep well, get that scheduled and have them come to do that early. This spot is a bust if they can't find water and there is no other good source. There's no reason to sink more money or energy into it. Provided that goes well (no pun intended), carry on! If you don't have a mailbox, you will want to get a P.O. box to receive mail and packages.

STEP FOUR: MAKE A SHELTER

Move to your new place. You're going to need a place to sleep. It's fine to start with something small like a camper, a trailer, or even a van if you can stand it. It's definitely recommended that you start in the spring when the temperature is just starting to warm up, and you have more warm months to get started.

If you have a family, they don't all have to come at this point. They can hang back while you get things prepared. It might require some trips back and forth; it might be a process.

Step Four can stay with the temporary place, or you can build a more permanent system as you go along. Step Four also fits between every other step.

STEP FIVE: GET YOUR BASELINE

You have a temporary shelter. You also need electricity, water, and food.

Get yourself a gas-powered generator. This is a temporary power source just until you can get your sustainable system operational.

You need water. You can have it delivered, or you can haul it yourself.

Food will be the same grocery-bought stuff you always use.

You'll also need a place to relieve yourself. If you have a trailer or a camper, that's covered. If not, you will need a bucket full of sawdust or an outhouse for the time being.

Garbage can be put in a can or bags and taken to the dump as needed.

Depending on how far out your new home is, you may not be able to catch a signal. You need to get some kind of communication system up as quickly as possible. You can buy a signal booster and attach it to a small tower. That can give you a lot more range. If that doesn't do the trick, consider getting a satellite Internet service.

You're going to want to be able to call for help in an emergency, check the weather, and look up how-to guides when you run into things you don't know how to do. Communication is mandatory.

You now have your baseline. You have all the basic needs covered. As this project continues, each one of those will be replaced with a sustainable system.

STEP SIX: ELECTRICITY

Set up your electrical system. You need your solar panels and/or wind turbines up. You need to get them hooked up safely.

You need a location to house the power system. That probably means building a shed to house everything away from the elements, especially water.

Run your connections from your power source. Hook up your AC inverter, batteries, charge controller, fuses, bus bars, etc. Get that all wired up. Contact an electrician if you need to. Safety first!

STEP SEVEN: WATER

Now that you have power, you can operate pumps. Once you can have operational pumps, you can get water. Your next task is to hook up to your water source. You are in business if you have tanks/cisterns, pipes, and filters ready to go. If you have a house built, that means hooking that up.

Life just got a lot easier. Also, you can now heat your water, which is a big deal if you've been living without it for a little while.

STEP EIGHT: WASTE

Now that you have water, you can hook that up to a septic system. Congratulations if you were using a bucket before because you can now use a toilet!

STEP NINE: START YOUR FARM

Now that you have working water, you can start your farm and your composting.

Set up a garden and/or build a greenhouse, and get started on any planting.

If you are keeping animals, build them a coop, barn, fenced-in area, or whatever they need. You are really rolling now!

STEP TEN: DO WHATEVER YOU WANT

You should have all the basic ingredients for self-sustenance: shelter, electricity, water, and food. You can use a toilet and take a shower.

These may not be completely up and running quite yet—you may have hiccups. If necessary, there's no shame in supplementing yourself with visits to the store if you need to.

Where you go from here is entirely up to you. You may find that you want to start upgrading some new systems. You may find that one of the systems you've already built can be built better or optimized.

All the necessities are taken care of. What you do next is whatever you want to do!

CONCLUSION

Now that we're at the end of the book, you may have started working out a rough sketch of the home you want to build. Maybe you've got your ideal state narrowed down to a few. You've got some ideas about what your home will look like, how you think you can power it, and how to supply water to it.

That's good—get that rough sketch, but don't try to put the ink down on this paper in your imagination just yet. Once you get started, there are going to be a lot of changes and adaptations that you will make along the way. Don't get too hung up on a perfect and idealized version of your homestead. Instead, you and the land should meet each other halfway and figure it out together.

This book will not be nearly enough to teach you everything you should or want to know.

There is a lot more to raising chickens and growing tomatoes than we could possibly cover in these few pages. One of the most important things you should do is continue learning.

When you decide you want to set up your own AC converter but don't know the first thing about electricity, you will have to read another book about that. Just absorb as much as you can. There are so many other homesteaders and off-grid people out there. There are many forums full of people that are eager to talk to you and share tips. There are countless websites full of great information that can teach you a lot and point you in the right direction.

We know that you're curious about moving off-grid, but at this stage, you're probably more than curious. If you didn't like the idea or it didn't sound like it was for you, you probably would have stopped reading this book halfway through earlier, but because you read it from the front to the back, you're still interested.

If you are so interested and have the means and opportunity, We would definitely recommend that you take this on. This is not something we would encourage a half-interested person to do, but if you have made it to the conclusion of this book, you are feeling excited, and you are thinking about all the different projects that you could do and the only things you want to learn, then we say follow that instinct. Take it to its ultimate conclusion.

Find your own independence, self-reliance, and environmental consideration, and build yourself a place where you will be happy and free.

ONE LAST THING

We spend so much of our modern lives making things that only exist virtually. Many of us spend a third of our day operating computers. Money people collate tables and leverage financial instruments to make money. Software engineers write complex algebraic formulas to develop a cell phone app. Marketing people look at charts and figures that tell them what people want without ever talking to people.

So much of what we do isn't material. It exists as an abstraction. People are aching to do something real, tangible, and right here. You'll see it in little ways.

You see people taking on knitting as a hobby, which was formerly considered something that old women do, but young women have suddenly taken an interest in crocheting and other crafts—things that require physical contact.

People are suddenly taking up hobbies like ax throwing and bowhunting.

People get on the Internet and look at videos of people building furniture from scratch.

People start brewing their own beer at home.

People seem to be yearning for another era where people worked with their hands, and when they were done working, there was something tangible in front of them—something that they could be proud of. Instead of working a job and seeing numbers appear in a bank account so they can purchase objects made on the other side of the world, they just want to make something themselves and have it. They want to see the fruits of their own labor and hold on to it like a trophy or a memento—some kind of physical reminder that they can be proud of.

You can feel it too, can't you? Building a life off-grid is not weird. What's weird is living in tiny concrete boxes, stacked hundreds of feet tall, in a gray, concrete place where you see thousands of people walk past you every day, and you don't know a single one of them.

If you want to try something new—if you want to craft the environment into a place just for you—then you are like many others. Many of them are less smart and talented than you are. If they can do it, you can, too.

OFF GRID SOLAR POWER
Introduction

I'd put my money on the sun and solar energy. What a source of power!

—Thomas Edison

Solar power has evolved to become an environmentally friendly, renewable source of energy and an affordable and cost-saving source of power. Its applications are endless, and improvements in the cost and efficiency of solar systems have skyrocketed over the past decade to the point where it is cheaper globally to produce power using solar arrays than using coal.

Our sun truly is the source of all life and energy on the planet, and we would be doing such a disservice to the environment if we didn't get more energy directly from this source. Solar power is reliable and predictable. You can easily track it based on the sun's intensity to the point where clouds passing and blocking out the sun will cause a noticeable drop in the energy produced by solar panels.

Solar systems are relatively straightforward to design and install. Of course, this is compared to other sources of energy, such as hydroelectric, natural gas, diesel, coal, wind, and geothermal energy. Most of these are far more complex, require far more capital and resources, and are not renewable. A common misunderstanding is that making use of a backup diesel generator is cheaper than using solar. This is only the case for people who think of the capital cost of buying the equipment. The actual cost of ownership for anything is in both the capital and operational costs. When considering this, you can see that, over the space of, say, five to ten years, using a diesel generator is more costly. You have to refuel it, replace filters and oil, and provide any other services required to keep it operational. You are also stuck with the noise that they make as well as the fumes that go everywhere. Hardly what you want for an off-grid solution. Compare this to a solar system which, once installed, essentially only needs to be cleaned. That's about it when it comes to regular maintenance. Every once in a while, you may have a damaged fuse, or you may be unfortunate enough to have lightning strike your panels, but these occasions are very few and far between.

Solar systems also have the benefit of battery backup systems. This takes out the argument that you can only have power when the sun is shining, far from it. When the sun is shining, you can make use of the energy and charge your batteries simultaneously, then make use of the energy stored at night just as though you were making use of the utility electricity supply. It really starts to look attractive when you look closer at your return of investment (ROI) on a solar system. This is essentially the time it takes for the solar system to save you the money equivalent to what you paid for the system in the first place. It is not uncommon for these systems to have an ROI period of around seven years. For a system that you could have in place for 25 years, paying it off over seven years and then actively saving money for the next 18 years is mind-boggling.

This is especially true for residential solar systems. When you start to look closely at your monthly electricity bill and see the figures drop due to your newly installed solar system, you will wonder why you didn't install your own solar system years ago!

We are Small Print Press, and we are committed to helping you sustainably survive and thrive while ensuring together that the world is a better place for future generations to come. Our mission is to empower people to mitigate all risks of potential disasters for themselves and their loved ones while still enjoying life and without living in fear. Having an off-grid solar power system in place is essential when dealing with natural disasters or becoming more self-sufficient.

Furthermore, it is only logical to make use of renewable energy moving forward. When it comes to things such as fossil fuels, coal, and natural gasses, we are limited by the quantity of these products that exist on the earth. You can compare it to engaging in a hunter and gatherer lifestyle versus a subsistence farming lifestyle. As much as you move from place to place, hunting contributes to the desolation of food resources in each region you travel through. These resources will never be able to supplement their reserves based on how quickly we consume them. Ancient populations started ballooning, and the hunter and gatherer lifestyle stopped making sense. Raising animals and crops in a set location made more sense for feeding the population. Over time, people could continue to grow more crops and raise more domesticated animals to feed expanding populations. Relying on a dwindling wild animal population made less and less sense. Renewable energy makes sense because we are reducing our reliance on finite resources that are dwindling just as wild game would dwindle with an expanding hunter population.

We at Small Footprint Press are fully aware of the detrimental impact we are having on the environment. We are consuming resources that have an expiration date without a concrete plan to address this problem. Moreover, we are burning fossil fuels to support our lifestyles and expanding global population while having unequivocal evidence that this behavior affects our climate and results in weather conditions that have significant consequences for our longevity on this planet. We want to create a lifestyle that is not destructive to our own lives and the ecosystems on this planet. It's often easy to forget that the tens of thousands of other species that live in this world have been here since long before we came around. These diverse animals, plants, fungi, birds, reptiles, bacteria, and everything in between all live on earth with us. We are still animals, just the same as they are. The only thing separating us is our intellect and recognition of others as individuals with their own conscience and thinking capability. We cannot continue on the path we are walking down because it will push us into a mass extinction event, which some already proclaim that we are in. This will escalate until all living things as we know them will die or change, and, most importantly, we will die off as well. However, the world will continue on. Life will continue on. We need to look past our greed to ensure our survival and longevity on earth.

It's not all gloom and doom, as we have been given the opportunity to make a change in our lifestyle. Although it may seem like a drop in the ocean to change your personal energy usage, if millions of people share the same mentality, then the power is with us. We are one with this world and need it to thrive for us to thrive. Our impact on the environment is unquestionable when looking at all evidence provided by science. We need to be more responsible and conscious. If we change by accelerating the transition to sustainable living and generating our own renewable energy for consumption, we are taking a step in the right direction.

Don't be disheartened by people telling you that the raw materials for solar systems require fossil fuels and that it negates its impact on the global climate, as these claims have been clearly debunked. It has been conclusively proven that solar panels themselves, made up of silicon, glass, copper, and aluminum, require at most two years of operation to generate as much power as was required to produce them (Svarc, 2019). The same can be said for lithium-ion batteries, which is a hot topic of discussion. Arguments arise from the mining of lithium, which is less labor and energy-intensive than the mining of aluminum. For the most part, lithium is a byproduct of other processes, such as brines, which account for half of all lithium produced from manufacturers. This means that the energy required to produce lithium-ion batteries could be provided using power generated by lithium-ion batteries, and it would still be productive energy. Essentially, it is an energy positive product, meaning that more energy can be generated from its extraction from the earth than would be consumed by extracting it (Talens Peiró et al., 2013). If you are ever confronted by people who argue that your solar system is more harmful to the environment than it benefits it, be sure to offer them these scientifically proven facts.

This book will go over all of the concepts around solar systems and how you can install your own. It will cover the basic overview of what solar power is, how you can design an effective solar system, and help you choose from all the different products out there in the market. You will be taken through some concepts around electricity so that, even if you have no knowledge in this field, you will be capable of installing your own solar system. We want to highlight now, and will do so again consistently in this book, the importance of safety whenever working with electricity. It is still very dangerous at the end of the day, so you must take the correct precautions, wear personal protective equipment (PPE), and follow the best practices. PPE consists of clothing designed to protect you. When installing and testing your solar system, insulated gloves and safety boots are the most important items to protect yourself from injury.

It is also important to inform you that there are laws and standards around using solar systems, particularly when you are interconnected with your electricity supplier. This book will cover some of the basics, but they vary from state to state and country to country. They are in place for a reason, and it isn't difficult to ensure that you comply with them and work with them to make sure that you have the best system possible.

If, on the other hand, you are installing a completely off-grid solution, then you only need to follow standards and safety precautions for your own benefit and don't necessarily need to register with your electricity supplier. It is a positive thing to see various laws and standards being processed by electricity suppliers because it shows that they support consumers making use of solar as much as possible. This book will focus on the small-scale, off-grid solar systems that you can install yourself. The primary focus areas will be in Recreational Vehicles (RV's), cabins, tiny homes, cars, boats, and other residential areas, such as larger homes. There are many similarities in how the systems work. The main difference is in the physical scale, installation procedures, and specific products necessary for particular applications, such as water-tight units for boat applications.

In the twenty-first century, there is a renewed drive for people to become more self-reliant and sustainable. You can reduce your carbon footprint, help the environment, save money, reduce your risk of calamities and generate your own clean energy to use however you choose. The only thing it requires is time, energy, and initial capital cost. Other than that, there is absolutely nothing to lose in installing your very own solar system. By the end of this book, you will be fully equipped to do it yourself!

Chapter 1: Solar Power Explained

In this chapter, we will cover the concepts behind solar power and how it is possible to capture solar energy. We will discuss the terminology that you can expect to come across and the various components that make up a solar-powered installation. Don't get disheartened if it seems like a lot to take in. Over time, you will realize that solar systems are straightforward and not overly complex. This makes it the perfect DIY project to pursue.

This chapter should give you a good background on how to go about designing, installing, and testing a solar system, as well as the basics of what it entails. It isn't an overload of information and lets you know what you are getting into when installing your own solar system. In the following chapters, we will expand more on concepts, theories, and how the various components work and are integrated with one another.

What is Solar Power and How Does it Work?

Lying at the center of our solar system is a gigantic, burning fusion reactor: the sun. Every second of every day, hydrogen is converted into helium on a massive scale, releasing heat, light, and energy. The light the sun releases arrives on earth in the form of photons. Each photon carries energy, and solar power is our way of harnessing that energy (Marsh, 2019). Solar power is harvested from what is known as solar irradiance. This essentially means that the more intense the sunlight is, the more energy it carries with it. This means that you can harness more energy per solar panel in light-intense areas.

It is interesting to note that humans are not the first species to harness the energy from the sun. Most plants use photosynthesis to convert carbon dioxide and water into carbohydrates with energy from the sun. It is a process necessary for life as we know it on the planet. The earliest form of humans using energy from the sun was to light fires using a magnifying method well over one and a half millennia ago. This has changed a great deal over the years, and solar energy now makes up an estimated 2% of the world's total energy usage (Ritchie & Roser, 2020). There are countless opportunities to elevate this quantity over the next decade as the world moves toward using more green energy and less energy generated from fossil fuels. The efficiency of converting energy from the sun into useful energy is not very high based on today's technology. This is not a cause of major concern, as even plants have a very low efficiency of using sunlight in the process of photosynthesis. As technology improves, our ability to absorb more energy will inevitably improve. The sun has been providing us with energy for billions of years. As humans, improving our ability to harness the sun is a testament to our initiative to seek out energy resources that will not run out or do major harm to our environment or communities living here.

The natural phenomena on earth are the main driving force behind generating more sustainable forms of electricity. We do need to consider the effects of drawing energy from natural forces such as hydroelectric power, as this may result in water channels being cut off when building dam walls. But, in cases such as wind power, tidal power from wave action in coastal areas, solar power, and geothermal energy, we are not impacting the environment in any measurable way. The wind will continue to blow in its course and have the same impact on the biosphere as we know it. Tides will continue to flow, and waves will continue to crash in coastal areas whether we harness this power or not. Geothermal heat will continue to be generated due to tectonic motion and pressure built up in the earth's crust, making use of this heat not harming the environment. The same goes for solar energy, which will strike the earth the same way it always has. The primary area of concern with any of these technologies is the energy required to get the raw materials necessary for the products that harness this energy.

Although there are areas of concern, such as inhumane working conditions for mine workers in many developing countries globally, most companies providing the raw materials have a strict ethical policy that seeks to improve and uplift communities surrounding mining areas. There are bad apples and those who will take advantage of communities or individuals, which is why transparency in major mining companies is required. We should never stop pressing these corporations to ensure that they can source raw materials such as copper, lithium, aluminum, and other raw materials ethically. These activities not doing more damage to the environment is just as important as the benefit gained in using them. If it uses more energy to extract lithium from the earth, then why would we use it in batteries as an energy storage method? It wouldn't make sense to burn more fossil fuels in extracting the products needed. All major manufacturers are aware of this, and it would make their product non-profitable, so scientific research is always ongoing to ensure that the direction we are moving in makes sense. There is no scientific evidence that extracting required raw materials outweighs the energy-saving capability of these products, so be sure not to alter your perception based on people who do not have any factual basis for their claims. The age of misinformation is upon us, and the only way to educate ourselves is to do our own research, look at the evidence and facts that are proven, and push to get answers in areas that we aren't certain about.

HOW CAN YOU HARNESS SOLAR POWER?

There are two ways in which we are able to generate electricity using energy from the sun. Thermal capturing is used far less for small-scale power generation and is only used in large-scale power generation plants. From the word thermal, you should recognize that this is a form of generating energy from the heat that is provided by the sun. There are also passive ways in which you can use this energy.

Solar thermal capturing is typically split into three categories: low, mid and high temperature. Low-temperature capturing is typically used in heating and cooling, mostly in buildings and living spaces. It is passive, and an example is letting natural light into your house for warmth in the winter and blocking the sun to keep a cool inside temperature during summer. The second form of solar thermal capturing is in mid temperatures. An example of this would be in using solar geysers. Heat is captured in collectors, and the heat energy is transferred to water in the geyser itself. It is a self-circulating system and a massive cost saver compared to geysers using electrical or gas elements. Finally, there are high-temperature solar thermal capturing systems. An example of this system would be concentrated solar plants that reflect sunlight using an array of reflector panels and focus it on tubes containing a fluid that absorbs thermal energy efficiently. The high amount of concentrated sunlight provides a large amount of heat absorbed by the fluid and used to turn water into steam and drive a turbine.

The other method of converting energy from the sun into electricity is using the photovoltaic process. The type of solar systems that we will focus on in this book are solar panels that make use of this process. All small-scale solar systems that generate electricity for homes, cabins, RV's, boats, and other vehicles use these solar panels. This is why many solar systems are referred to as photovoltaic (PV) arrays. It's helpful to understand this jargon and recognize why it is used. An array is a description of several panels mounted together to generate power.

HOW DO SOLAR PANELS CONVERT SOLAR ENERGY INTO USABLE ELECTRICITY?

There are two predominant ways in which energy from the sun can be harnessed to produce energy that is beneficial to us. The first of these methods, as I briefly discussed above, involves solar thermal energy capturing. Common procedures used to provide a function from this form of energy harvesting are solar geysers and solar concentrate plants. Solar geysers are mounted in order to absorb heat from the sun and used to circulate and heat water for usage, saving the electricity from using standard electrical and gas geysers, which require burning gas to heat water for cleaning, showering, and other practical purposes (Hutchison & Galiardi, 2019).

Another larger-scale example of making use of the thermal energy from the sun is concentrated in a solar plant. In these systems, hundreds of solar panels face a central tower, and this focused beam of light is used to superheat a solution that has been designed to retain heat very well.

A final form of this energy is in parabolic solar power plants. In these systems, solar panels are mounted in a c-shape, or parabola. These panels have a central line with water inside that is mounted at the focus point of the solar panels. The heat energy from the sun is focused on this central line, which typically carries water or another liquid that absorbs heat efficiently and can be superheated. The heat is then transferred to generate power. These systems are cheaper, as no cells are needed, only reflectors. They also have the advantage of not having a dependency on temperature and have a much longer lifespan than standard solar panels. However, they are far less energy efficient, still require cleaning, and take up a lot of physical space.

The other form of solar generation is the photovoltaic process. This is the process that typical solar systems use. When sunlight strikes the solar cells, typically made up of a semiconductive material such as silicon, it dislodges the semiconductor's electrons. These electrons are set in motion and flow to an area with a more positive charge. This is because electrons carry a negative charge and move to an area with a more positive charge via attraction. Likewise, the location where the electron starts becomes more negatively charged, this repels the electron away. In other words, a potential difference is set up between the electron's existing position and a more positive location, which results in the electrons moving and creating a flow of current. When the cells are connected in series, the potential difference across the cells increases while the flow of current through each cell remains the same. This boosts the power and is the reason why typical solar panels are the size that they are. They are small enough to be handled by a single person, easily replaceable, and robust enough in their manufacturing. They are also large enough to have each panel generate a significant amount of power. It would be more costly to build solar panels that are the size of a single cell, as more materials would be needed to build frames, increasing the cost of each unit significantly.

OFF-GRID VS. ON-GRID (AKA GRID-TIED) SOLAR ENERGY

There are two main types of solar arrays: off-grid and on-grid solar systems. To explain the difference between the two, we need to look at what is meant by "the grid." The electrical grid is the network of electrical infrastructure that connects all parts of a country, or even several countries, together. It includes generation, where energy is first produced; transmission, which is similar to the arteries transporting power to different parts of a country or country; and distribution, which takes electricity to every end-user. This electrical network is typically termed as the grid. There are standards, including quality and safety standards, that come with being tied into the grid. If you receive your power from a utility, then you are connected to the grid.

In terms of a solar system, if your solar system is connected to the grid in any way, then it is a grid-tied solution. A grid-tied solar system may or may not have a battery backup system, as you receive power from both your solar panels and the grid. This means that you don't necessarily require batteries. You need to register your solar system and have it approved by your electricity supplier. The main reason for this is that electricity suppliers need to know all the power sources on the grid. If you have a grid-tied solution, when the grid supply fails and you aren't supplied by them anymore, your system has to disconnect from the grid automatically. You can still supply power to yourself, but you cannot be connected to the grid. The reasoning behind this is simple enough. If power is turned off to a section of the grid where there is a fault, there can be nothing making that section live for safety reasons. If you haven't disconnected from the grid, you may make a grid section that needs to be worked on live. This would carry the risk of someone getting electrocuted and hurt because they are unaware of a power source. If the section is isolated, it should be safe to work on, and if it is isolated and the section is still found to be live, then figuring out where the power is coming from can waste time for those fixing the fault (August 12 & 2019, 2019).

The second option for a solar system is to have an off-grid system. In this system, the electrical network that you create is completely separate from the primary grid. You generate your own power and use it up while not connecting to the main electrical network. The advantage of this solution is that you can install your own backup battery system and be completely independent of the utility supply. In the long run, both systems will save you money. However, by using an off-grid system, the initial capital expense may be more than a grid-tied system, as you will probably need a larger solar system and would have to rewire several electrical connections. Still, in the long run, it will save you more money. This is partly because you will not be paying your monthly electricity usage, but also because you will not have to pay a maximum demand surcharge or a levy to have a connection to the utility.

THE FOUR MAIN COMPONENTS OF A SIMPLE OFF-GRID SOLAR POWER SYSTEM

A typical off-grid solar-powered system consists of four primary components: solar panels, battery chargers, batteries, and power inverters. Each of these four components plays a vital role and works together to provide you with electricity that you can use. Other smaller components come into play, and we will get into the details of these in Chapter 2.

The solar panels are the power source of a solar system. Each panel comprises dozens of photovoltaic cells that work together and generate direct current (DC) power. They are often termed modules, panels, or solar panels. They are connected either parallel or in a series to create what is described as a solar array. A solar array generates electricity at a suitable DC voltage and current for the inverter to convert to alternating current (AC). These are two different types of electricity, and some devices can convert electricity from one type to another. The description of these two different types of electricity, AC and DC, is included in Chapter 2 below.

The second component in a solar system is the battery chargers or charge controllers. When it comes to these units, there are several options to connect to the system. There are charge controllers that use the DC electricity generated by the solar panels and charge batteries directly from this power source. There are also battery chargers that can be connected after the inverter, which charge and manage your batteries. The final option is with certain brands of inverters that have a built-in battery charger. The purpose of the battery chargers is to enable power to flow to the batteries when they are charging and from the batteries when they are discharging. Batteries are able to store energy, but must be carefully charged with energy and discharged of stored energy. The battery chargers also need to protect the batteries from being damaged by short circuits or power surges. The main reason for this is that batteries are one of the most expensive solar system components.

The third component is the batteries themselves. There are a whole host of battery types that can be used, but their function remains the same. Batteries are designed to store energy by being charged when surplus power is generated by the solar panels, such as when the sun is shining. They are then used as the source of power when insufficient energy is supplied by the solar array, such as at night. Making use of batteries creates a stable and consistent power supply from your solar system. It is proposed to oversize your solar system, especially your battery backup because you cannot predict whether you will use more power than expected or if the weather will not be conducive to generating power consistently. If you have several days of cloudy weather, then your solar panels will not be able to generate as much power compared to when it is sunny. This means that the solar panels will not meet the energy demand that you have. If you have an undersized battery backup system, then you may get by for a few days, but once the batteries have been discharged, you will be left with no power at all!

The final component of your solar system is the inverter. Inverters are devices that convert electricity from DC to AC. AC is the form of electricity that is used in all typical households. Therefore, to use the type of power that devices make use of, you need to convert the type of power that solar panels generate. Inverters use semiconductors to convert electricity and typically have a filter that gives you good quality AC supply that is safe to connect all devices to. In the US, that supply is 110 volts (V) at a frequency of 60 hertz. In many other countries worldwide, the supply power is 230 V at a frequency of 50 hertz. The type of inverter you use depends on your region and what power is used.

These four main components work in unison to give you a fully functional solar system. The solar panels, or modules, generate power from sunlight, the batteries are charged with a battery charger, the batteries themselves store energy to be used when required, and the inverter converts the electricity to the standard electrical supply used in that region.

It is important to note that, beyond these four primary components that make up your solar system, there are also many more minor but still important things you will need to specify, design for, purchase, and install with your solar system. It is also of great importance that you thoroughly test your solar system to pick up on any defects or errors in how your system is set up and installed. Of course, it is far easier and cheaper to check for problems before you install your system at all, so making use of calculations and simulation software can greatly assist you in planning your system out. On average, you should go through three major phases in implementing your solar system, and each of these phases will take approximately the same amount of time.

PHASES OF INSTALLATION

The first phase is in designing your system. This includes determining where you want to install your solar system, how you want to go about the installation, and specifying the various components that you require. This includes sizing your solar panels as individual units and establishing the total number of panels that you will require. It also includes your batteries, inverter, battery charger or charge controller, tools, mounting equipment, wires, and safety practices that you should follow all the way through. You should carry out all your calculations and test your system using some form of software simulation. There are numerous software with free 30 day trials available to test if your system will work in the way you hope it will. This whole process can be called the planning phase.

The second part of your solar project is purchasing and adjudicating. You will have to research what solar panels, batteries, inverters, and charge controllers are available to you. There is no point in designing for an inverter that is readily available in Germany but extremely expensive with an extended delivery time to get to you in the US. There may also be several options that seem almost identical, and this is where you will need to adjudicate. It could be as simple as a pros and cons list to compare two different products in order to choose the best option for you. It could have a major impact on you if you go with a cheap option, only to discover later that many of the features you require do not come with the inverter or have to be purchased separately. During this phase, you should be able to narrow down your options and purchase them from suppliers. It is imperative that you get the installation manuals with these products to ensure that you follow the manufacturer's specifications on installing the products. This phase will often lead you to a point where you realize that something you had designed for in stage one is not practically feasible, and you will have to go back to tweak your design. There is nothing wrong with this, and you shouldn't feel disheartened if you go back more than once to adjust your design to match what is available to you on the market. It's an iterative process that you want to complete in this stage, preferably before you actually purchase the equipment.

The third and final stage is the installation and testing of your solar system. If you have managed to plan out your layout, equipment, and installation method, then things should go fairly smoothly. However, in practice, there are always things that you may have missed: a tool you may require, more wires, connectors, screws, or drill bits. Nothing will ever go entirely according to plan, but the better you have planned, the fewer headaches you will have during this stage. This is often termed teething problems in engineering because a new installation will give you more trouble than a system operating for a long time. You must prepare yourself for teething problems and remain attentive to them. Sometimes, it could be something minor, such as your solar panels being dirty or a fuse blowing when you first started testing your system. Other times, the problems are a bit more challenging to overcome, such as your solar panels not being installed correctly or a large tree casting a shadow over half of your solar panels.

In this final stage, you will also need to test and monitor how your system is operating. You can use clamp meters to measure current and multimeters to measure voltage to confirm that the power you are generating is in line with what you designed for. You will also need to test any safety devices, such as isolating your solar system safely for maintenance or replacements needed later on.

These three stages form the lifecycle of your solar project and, if you follow them, spend an equal amount of time on each phase, and don't skip any major steps, then your system will be successful. You will be fully geared up to generate your own electricity, save a lot of money in the long run, and always have a backup power source should the grid go down.

CHAPTER 2:
ELECTRICITY 101

This chapter will go over general electricity concepts to make sense of solar systems and how to go about designing and installing them. By the end of this chapter, you should grasp the basic aspects of electricity that are relevant to solar systems.

BASIC FORMS OF POWER

To start, let us cover the two different types of electricity. These were mentioned in Chapter 1 and are known as AC and DC. AC has a voltage that alternates from positive to negative due to the charge of electrons when the power is generated, which is driven by the magnetic field. There are north and south poles of a magnet which result in the positive and negative charge. AC is named as such because the flow of electrons alternates between positive and negative. A sinusoidal wave flows along the path of electricity from the power source to where the power is used. Picture it as a wave that is generated when you throw a pebble into a pond. The waves flow away from where the pebble hits the water, and any single point experiences the water rising and falling as it moves past it. In the same way, AC electricity flows away from the power source to where the power is used. It is more straightforward to transmit AC over long distances, and it is the form of electricity that is in every household.

The other type of electricity, DC, has a continuous charge, and the voltage remains more or less stable. Instead of a wave, it is flat. DC is more stable, particularly at low voltage; therefore, many appliances and electronics use DC.

The next aspects of electricity that we will cover are that of voltage, current, and resistance:

Voltage is measured in volts and is defined as the potential difference between two points. For example, in a car battery, the potential difference between the positive and negative terminal is 12 Volts. Voltage is the driving force behind electricity. One volt is the potential difference between two points on a wire, where one ampere of current dissipates one watt of power. This may sound confusing, but it will make sense once we cover the other aspects.

- The voltage, or potential difference, is the driving force pushing the electrons from one point to another, and the term used to describe this flow of charge is termed as the current. Thus, the current describes the rate of flow of charge from one point to another.

- The ampere, or amp for short, is the measure of current flow in electricity. In order for electricity to flow, there needs to be an exchange of electrons from one point to another. This essentially means that there is a flow of charged particles from one point to another, which is electricity.

- The next term to look into is resistance. Resistance is measured in ohms, and it resists the flow of current due to a potential difference. If it weren't for resistance in materials, we would have perfect conductors and no electricity losses. Resistance essentially takes the energy that is transmitted via electricity and wastes some of it, typically in the form of heat.

A simple way to understand the concept of these three interacting aspects of electricity is to use an analogy of something that is easier to visualize than electricity. The most common and most straightforward analogy used is that of water flowing through a pipe. In terms of water moving through a pipe, voltage is the pressure of the water, the current is the flow rate, and the diameter of the pipe is the resistance. The higher the pressure is, the faster the flow rate will be. Similarly, if there is a higher potential difference or a larger voltage, there will be an increased flow of current. The voltage would be an increase of water pressure, resulting in increased water flow given the right conditions. Do not get confused when seeing the description of potential difference and voltage used interchangeably in datasheets and other documentation, as they are the same thing when referring to electricity. However, the diameter of the pipe will limit the flow of water. A more narrow pipe represents a higher resistance. In this instance, higher pressure is required for the same flow rattan to a setup with a wider diameter pipe.

The next concept that needs to be presented is that of electrical power. Power is measured in watts and is determined by the current and voltage of a system. To calculate the power, you only need to multiply the current and the voltage. The power determines how much energy is being transferred from the source to the load at any given time. For example, if a 12 V battery is driving a 2 A current across a load, then the power delivered to the load is the two multiplied by each other, or 24 W.

THE DIFFERENCE BETWEEN POWER AND ENERGY

The power measured in watts describes how much energy is used up at any given time, so when you see a light bulb that is 100 W, you know that it uses more energy every second than a 60 W light bulb. Total energy use is calculated by multiplying the power supplied in one moment by the amount of time power was supplied. However, this is different from how most energy meters work. When you receive an electrical bill, the amount of energy you use is not given to you in the units of energy, which is joules. It seems unusual that you aren't charged for the exact amount of energy you used, so why is that?

The short answer is that it is too complicated to measure the power flow at every single instance and determine its energy. Instead, what is used is referred to as watt-hours (Wh). When you are charged from your utility, the bill will typically describe the energy used up as kilowatt hours (kWh). A kilo represents a unit of 1,000, so 1,000 Wh is the same as 1 kWh. We are all charged in kWh from the utility because this is an average amount of energy that we use and not the precise amount itself. Typically, energy meters sample the amount of power being used once every 15 minutes. This means that four samples are taken over the span of an hour, and they all contribute to the overall amount of energy estimated (Enphase, n.d.).

An analogy to describe the difference between watts and watt-hours, which is essentially the difference between power and energy, is looking at speed and distance. Power is the rate of flow of energy, just as speed is the rate of change of distance. So, if you are driving at 60 mph, that would be equivalent to the power. If you were to drive for 30 minutes at this speed in a single direction, then you should cover 30miles, and this would be the equivalent of the energy. The faster you go, the more distance you can cover. Similar to the higher power you have, the more energy you can transfer.

When it comes to batteries, the measurement of energy available is typically provided in ampere-hours (Ah). This, again, can be translated into energy, as energy is the product of power and time. If, for example, you have a car battery, which is typically 12 V, and are given a rating of 200 Ah as the battery rating, then you can determine the energy stored by multiplying amp hours by the voltage, so 200 x 12, which is 6,000 Wh of 6 kWh of energy. The reason for this type of measurement is that it makes it easier to determine how long your batteries last. If you have the same 200 Ah battery and have several devices that you wish to power from it, you only need to look at how much current these devices draw to know how long the battery will last. For example, if you have lights and some devices connected to plugs and you work out that you will need 20 A of current, you only need to determine how much power you can draw from the battery. Theoretically, a battery being rated at 200 Ah should be able to supply 20 A for 10 hours. This will be covered in more detail in Chapter 2 when we discuss deep cycles for batteries.

Another important feature of electrical systems is protection. Protection is self-explanatory, and multiple protection devices are used to protect both people and electrical devices. Examples of protection devices are circuit breakers and fuses. When there is an electrical fault or a short circuit, these protection devices will be activated—circuit breakers trip to isolate the power to prevent any further damage or harm done to people. Think of them as a light switch that turns the power off automatically when it detects too much current flow to the load. When it comes to fuses, they will burn out instantly to open the circuit and stop the current from flowing when there is too much current flowing through them. Both fuses and circuit breakers typically have a rating that tells you how much current they will allow to flow through them and when they will operate to protect the electrical devices.

BASICS ON SOLAR SYSTEMS

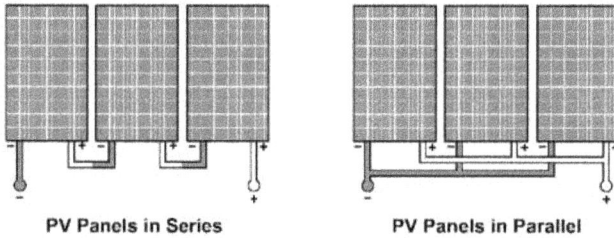

PV Panels in Series   PV Panels in Parallel

Now that we have covered some of the basic electricity terms, let's take a closer look at solar systems in particular and all the required components. You can connect panels to form what is called a string. A string of panels is typically made up of several panels connected in series. In electricity, the two main ways of connecting a circuit are called series-connected and parallel-connected components. A series connection links one component to another to form a big loop, whereas a parallel connection links components together like the steps of a ladder. All components are connected to the same line on each side.

When you connect a string of solar panels, if you opt for a DC charge controller, it is important to have fuses at the point of connection to the inverter and charge controller of the batteries.

These fuses will protect the inverter, battery charger, and other solar panels if there is a short circuit.

Strings of solar panels work together to increase the voltage and boost the amount of generated power. The more solar panels that you have, the more power you can generate. Most inverters are equipped with multiple inputs from the solar panels to allow several strings of panels to be connected.

There is also certain terminology that you will need to be familiar with regarding electrical infrastructure relating to your solar system. The first of these things is a distribution board (DB). This is basically where your power is distributed to the different loads. All houses have a DB with an incomer from the utility, metering of some kind for the utility to track and charge you for your electricity usage, and feeders that feed power to your home's different areas. The concept is the same for an off-grid solar system. All your AC power will have to be fed from this single location. DBs typically have an incomer from your power source, which will be your inverter in this case. The incomer is typically a circuit breaker that is often called your main breaker. You will then find smaller circuit breakers that feed the different areas that require power. Lights are usually fed from what is known as a single-pole circuit breaker, and plugs, geysers, stoves, and other major loads are fed from double pole circuit breakers. A double pole circuit breaker has both a live and neutral connection from the circuit breaker to the loads, whereas single pole circuit breakers only have the live connection.

There is also typically an earth leakage unit that is designed to protect from earth faults in your system, an earth bar, a neutral bar, and a protected neutral bar. An earth leakage device is a device that is designed to protect you from getting electrocuted. It detects the current flowing to a load and returning from it, as electricity has to circulate in a loop. If it is detected that the current flowing to your loads does not match the current flowing back from them, it is assumed that there is a discharge to earth through a person or device. This is hazardous and could potentially injure a person, so when this situation is detected, the power is isolated completely. A DB is sometimes called a fuse box or feeder panel depending on the size and functionality, but they refer to the same fundamental thing.

An inverter is a device that converts the DC power that is generated from your solar system or batteries into AC power for you to use for plug points, appliances, and lighting. They are one of the core components of your solar system, alongside the batteries, battery charger, and solar panels. Inverters make use of semiconductive devices, and they have a limit to their efficiency. Be careful when sizing your solar system, as the power generated by your solar panels will not be 100% available for you to use in your AC system. A good rule of thumb to use is to take an efficiency of 85%, meaning that, of the power generated by your solar panels, only 85% will be available to use. This will help you avoid any issues in the future when you realize that you aren't able to get as much power out of your solar system as you originally expected.

When it comes to solar systems, there is a term known as peak sun hours (PSH), which effectively allows you to calculate how much power you can get from your solar panels on an average day. Although there may be 12 hours of sunlight on an average day, you may only have a listing of seven hours of PSH, as your panels will not be generating 100% power over the full 12 hours. Instead, there may be five hours of fully efficient production of electricity and four hours of partial efficiency, resulting in only seven hours of full productivity. In the four hours of partial sun exposure, you may get approximately 50% of the sun intensity and photons you would receive during the middle of the day. This means that the four hours of 50% sun intensity translate to two hours of PSH.

When you determine the amount of power that you can get from your panels, you shouldn't use the number of hours of sunlight during the day, but, rather, the number of PSH. This is also important for seasonal changes as your panels will inevitably have fewer PSH during the winter months when compared to the summer months.

Another concept that isn't often discussed is the power factor. Power is technically measured as apparent power, also known as active power, which makes up the watts that we are now familiar with, and the second type of power is known as reactive power. Reactive power is a power that doesn't show active use and is a part of your power that you want to reduce as far as possible. All inductive loads, such as stoves and geysers, have a component of inductance that demands reactive power. This power isn't obviously shown in your active power or watt usage, making it confusing sometimes when you look at your power demand and solar system capability and see a gap between the two. It's not easy to explain, but the basics are that a voltage is set up, and the current follows it. The greater the lag between the voltage set up and the flow of current is determined by induction, and the further behind the current lags, the lower your power factor and the more power is lost without delivering useful energy. The most typical way that reactive power is compensated for is by using filter devices such as capacitors. They are commonly used in larger-scale electrical systems but are costly and are not used often in residential applications.

Solar inverters are designed to supply your load based on its requirements. If you have large inductive loads, the chances are that you will have what is known as a poor power factor. Power factor is basically a ratio between the different forms of power. A typical load will have a power factor ranging from 0 to 1.0. A value of 1.0 is outstanding. It means that your ratio of apparent power, measured in volt-amps (VA), is exactly equal to your active, or real, power with a ratio of one to one. It may seem confusing since the ratio is not linear and is a root mean squared ratio. That being said, a power factor of 0.8 is terrible, whereas a power factor of 0.95 is very good. This translates to 80% of your power being used in a useful way versus 95% of your power being used in a useful way.

This is an important aspect to cover because your inverters will put out power to cater to loads of a certain size, but that doesn't consider the type of load you are connecting. If you are unaware of this theory, then you may end up underestimating the size of your inverter, expecting it to power loads that it simply isn't adequate for. No system will have a perfect power factor; thus, a lot of the power that your inverter will generate goes into this "wasted" energy that hasn't been accounted for. When configuring your inverter, you will typically be able to see the amount of real and reactive power that you are generating but not be able to compensate for this. There are devices known as power factor correction banks, but these are designed more for larger-scale systems.

In terms of power factor for your solar system, just assume that it accounts for a reduction in efficiency between the power that your inverter can generate and the power demand of your load. In this way, it will not take you by surprise later on when you aren't getting out what you expected.

There is also an aspect known as insulation. The insulation of a material is the opposite of the conductivity. If something is a good insulator, then it is a very poor conductor and vice versa. This is specific to electricity in this case, as conductivity could be for several other things, such as heat. It is important to have good insulation materials for things that should not be live. This includes the insulation material that surrounds cables and all components that shield you from live conductors. How well a material can withstand and protect you from live conductors is known as the insulation voltage rating. This is different for AC and DC voltages, as explained below.

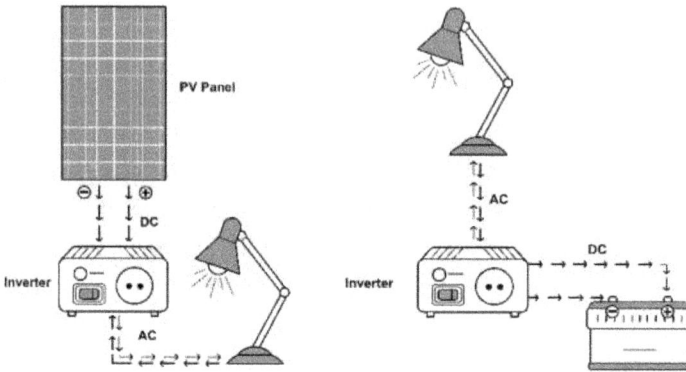

How Inverters Work

The process of converting DC power into AC power is known as inverting the power. The process of converting AC power into DC power is termed rectifying the power. When the process takes place, the voltage that you get on one side does not match the other side, i.e., 1 V of AC power does not become 1 V of DC power once it has been rectified. This is true for both the rectifying and inverting process. The DC voltage equivalent from rectifying AC can be calculated with the following simple equation:

Voltage Insulation Rating (DC) = Voltage Insulation Rating (AC) / 2

This implies that an insulation material that can protect you from 1,000V of AC power can only protect you from 700 V of DC power. It's important to know this difference so that you don't specify an insulator or any equipment with an insulation rating in AC and expect it to work for the same DC voltage.

Another aspect to consider with designing, purchasing, installing, and testing your solar system is to look at engineering firms that carry out these projects daily. There are many lessons that you can take from them when building your own system. It's easier to learn from other's mistakes or best practices than to have to go through the trouble yourself. One practice that is often skipped in do-it-yourself projects is having a design review of some kind. If you have designed your own system, you may not be aware of any gaps in your design or things that you may not have considered that are commonplace in solar systems. Engineering companies will hold internal reviews where a team of experts gives feedback on one person's design. The design will be scrutinized to determine whether the solution makes sense technically, legally, ethically, that it meets quality standards, and that it is, indeed, the best fit solution for the requirements at hand. A good idea is to discuss your design with someone who has carried out their own solar system before and get input. It can be expanded into getting multiple opinions on your design and plans. It isn't about changing your design completely because someone else has a different opinion on how you should do things. It is more of a guideline to help you think laterally and think of things that may have slipped through the cracks when you carried out the design of your system. Again, it is far easier and cheaper to make changes to your design before it has materialized than after!

CHAPTER 3: HOW TO CHOOSE THE RIGHT BATTERY

When it comes to figuring out which battery to use for your solar system, you need to know what different batteries are available on the market and the pros and cons of the different types of batteries. You may think you are getting a great deal on cheap batteries only to find that they don't perform well and only last you two to three years before failing. You may look at the price tag of a high-end battery and feel as though you are being ripped off only to find that it is a deep cycle battery that performs well and lasts you over ten years. It's all about selecting the best option for the right price.

It's important to remember, once again, that the cost of something isn't purely about the price tag that you see when you first purchase something. The cost of ownership should also be compared. If you have a maintenance-free battery, then you will save on maintenance costs. Also, if you have an expensive battery option that lasts you ten years and another is half the cost but only lasts for three years, you will save in the long run by going for the more expensive battery.

Let's begin by explaining what a deep cycle battery is. Batteries are basically devices that store energy. They require charging in order to absorb the energy. When this power is needed, the batteries discharge to supply the power. The process of charging and discharging is not perfect, and there are losses experienced. Due to the physical construction of batteries, they cannot be discharged to 0% charge. Standard batteries can only discharge to 60% charge, meaning that only 40% of the energy stored in the batteries can be accessed. Deep cycle batteries can discharge 80% of their stored energy, which is significantly more than standard batteries. However, in order to ensure that the lifespan of the batteries is per manufacturer specifications, you shouldn't discharge them beyond a 45% charge. If you stick to this, you will be able to use the batteries for a much longer time. When you discharge the battery to its limit, there is internal degradation of the batteries, which means that they will never be able to store as much energy as before. The more you cycle beyond the point specified, the more degradation will occur until the batteries will not be able to charge at all. This will inevitably happen with all batteries, but it is better to have batteries last for five years than overwork them and last only three years (Crown Battery, 2018).

When it comes to deep cycle batteries, you can cycle the charge and discharge amounts at a much higher rate than other battery types. Most batteries will also have a rated number of cycles guaranteed, which is an important factor to take into consideration when selecting a battery. Some will guarantee up to 500 cycles, which would result in less than two years of daily use. Others will guarantee as many as 2,500 cycles, meaning they will last you much longer even if you are discharging them more than once per day (Energy Matters, n.d.).

Two additional categories describe the different types of deep cycle batteries. These are sealed type, or maintenance-free batteries, and flooded deep cycle batteries. Flooded deep cycle batteries require inspection and maintenance. For lead-acid batteries, which are the most commonly used, there is a minimum and maximum level of electrolytic liquid. When the liquid drops below the minimum level, they need to be topped up with distilled water. Many batteries are described as sealed type batteries, but aren't truly sealed batteries. This is specifically true for absorbed glass mat (AGM) batteries, which are actually valve regulated and not truly sealed. In fact, most sealed type batteries are actually valve regulated. As another example, lead acid batteries give off hydrogen gas over time, specifically when they charge, and this gas builds up pressure in the batteries. This is why, instead of being completely sealed, these batteries have a valve to allow the gas to be released before the internal pressure gets to a dangerous level.

There are also different types of batteries that work using different principles. The most common types of batteries used for energy storage are lithium-ion, flooded lead-acid, AGM, and gel batteries. Each of these primary types of batteries have pros and cons, which are essential to know for you to decide what will best fit your requirements.

LITHIUM-ION BATTERIES

Lithium-ion batteries are one of the most commonly used batteries used today. They are lightweight compared to other batteries, which explains why they are used in many electronic devices such as cell phones, tablets, and laptops. They are incredibly durable and are more resilient to harsh weather conditions than other batteries. They also last the longest of the five battery types mentioned above, and they require very little or no maintenance at all. The batteries themselves are sealed, so it is mostly the connections that need to be checked once in a while to see if the battery is still charging and discharging adequately. The batteries are also compact and don't take up a lot of space, which is great when this is a factor to consider, such as in an RV or on a boat.

The disadvantage when it comes to lithium-ion batteries is that they are costly. A typical, deep-cycle lithium-ion battery will cost about four times as much as the other options that will be discussed. That being said, they will last the longest out of all of the batteries, with many being rated to last between 10 and 15 years. Another drawback with lithium-ion batteries is that they are sensitive to electrical faults and need to be protected against them, particularly voltage surges. They are also sensitive to temperature and will not last as long in high temperatures (above 25 degrees Celsius, or 77 degrees Fahrenheit). This means that they need to be stored in a cool, dry area to maximize their lifespan. Another issue comes with disposing of lithium-ion batteries. If a lithium-ion battery is pierced, it can be explosive. This is why manufacturers of lithium-ion batteries take every precaution possible to ensure any failure is sealed by having protective plates. However, if these batteries were to end up in a dump, the risk increases. This means that, after the batteries stop working, there is a small expense for specialists to dispose of them responsibly.

FLOODED LEAD ACID BATTERIES

The next battery that we will look at is the flooded lead acid battery. As previously mentioned, they do require regular inspection and maintenance. They have been around for a long time and are known to be reliable hence car batteries today still make use of lead acid batteries. They are also used in battery tripping units in almost every substation in the world for backup power to protect devices connecting the grid.

One of the most significant advantages of these types of batteries is that they can supply a large amount of power quickly without damage to the batteries. If you turn on a device with an element such as a kettle, geyser, or toaster, the power drawn spikes as a large amount of current is needed to power these devices. These batteries are able to supply this demand without it affecting the quality of the power being delivered. They are also cheap in comparison to the other types of batteries on this list. If you have several different large loads that you will be turning on and off regularly, these batteries may be the option you are looking for. Although these batteries require maintenance, they have a relatively simple design and are easy to repair.

The disadvantage with these batteries is that they contain a liquid with a cap keeping the liquid in, but they need to be kept upright, and it is not advisable to move them often. Although they typically have a cap to keep the liquid from spilling over, it is not a vacuum seal, and the electrolytic liquid will leak if the batteries are moved often. Also, as mentioned, they require frequent inspection and topping up with distilled water when the electrolytic liquid drops below the minimum threshold. They also have a low energy density, meaning that they don't store a large amount of energy for their physical size and weight. This type of battery also gives off hydrogen gas as they charge, which is flammable. This isn't a problem when they are stored in an area with good ventilation, but if they are stored in a sealed room, the buildup of hydrogen can be dangerous.

These batteries also have the risk of chemical burns as they do contain acid. It is crucial that these batteries are stored upright so as not to leak this acidic electrolytic liquid. The term "electrolytic", for the liquid contained in batteries, is used because these batteries use a process known as electrolysis to store a charge. When the batteries are charging, electrolysis occurs, which converts the chemicals into ions and anions, which are the batteries' positive and negatively charged elements. These then combine to form a single compound, and this process is used to store and release energy. Chemical processes require energy. In certain chemical processes, energy is released when different elements combine. This change of energy levels is what is analyzed when determining what compounds could potentially make for good batteries. Other conditions are considered as well when selecting what chemicals to make use of in batteries. Such as the chemical process taking place at room temperature, how easy it is to reverse the process, and whether or not degradation can be minimized so the chemical process can be reversed and repeated many times. Batteries are chemical reactions in a mostly closed system and store and release energy in the form of electricity when we require it.

There is also the risk of thermal runaway where the batteries are overused and overheat, which results in dangerously high temperatures for the electrolytic material. This is an extremely infrequent occurrence, and battery manufacturers design their batteries to reduce this risk as far as practically possible. If your batteries are not operating correctly and are running hot, then it is highly recommended that you remove them from the operation. This rare occurrence will occur when there is a defect in a battery; therefore, if this were to happen to one of your batteries, it would likely only be in one of the batteries in your battery bank. A warranty claim can almost always be made in this instance, provided you are storing your batteries correctly and in accordance with the manufacturer's specifications.

VALVE REGULATED OR SEALED BATTERIES

The final battery is the valve regulated, or sealed, battery. These come in two main forms: AGM and gel type batteries. Unlike the flooded lead acid batteries, these units are self-contained and require no real maintenance, only an inspection from time to time. The most significant advantage of these batteries is that they can hold their charge for a very long time, unlike most batteries which discharge over time. Think of a car that has been standing for a few weeks, but it still has enough charge to start the car. That ability to hold charge while not being used over extended periods of time is a massive benefit with these batteries. This makes them ideal for solar systems that aren't used daily, such as in RVs. They are self-contained and give off only trace amounts of hydrogen over time. They are also significantly cheaper than lithium-ion batteries, which are also sealed batteries that do not spill. The final advantage of these batteries is that they are non-hazardous, making them safer to dispose of than lithium-ion batteries.

One of the disadvantages associated with these batteries is that they are more expensive than flooded lead acid batteries. They also don't last as long as lithium-ion batteries, resulting in their demand decreasing over time. They are bulkier than lithium-ion batteries and have a shorter lifespan.

AGM batteries, in particular, are incredibly robust and can handle movement and shock. This is why they are used as car batteries in almost all internal combustion engine vehicles. These batteries can also charge to a full charge at a lower voltage than specified. This means that even a 12 V rated battery can be fully charged with a 10 V supply voltage, which is hugely advantageous. They can also handle the high current without being damaged. AGM batteries can be charged quicker than other batteries and can give a deep cycle discharge when power is needed. This makes them just as popular as lithium-ion batteries for solar solutions, especially when it comes to mobile applications such as RV's, boats, and trailers for camping.

Gel batteries, like AGM batteries, are robust and resistant to shock and are also maintenance-free apart from inspections. They also have the advantage of not leaking even if their physical construction is compromised. They are incredibly resilient in extreme temperatures, making them functional even in extreme weather conditions, such as low or high temperatures, high humidity, or high altitude. These batteries can be transported without issues and operate normally, even when on their side or upside down. Because of their extreme resilience to extreme weather, they are often used in marine and aircraft applications.

However, gel batteries are not as popular when it comes to solar solutions because they are far more expensive than AGM batteries with similar properties. They are also extremely sensitive to how they are charged and can be damaged easily electrically, despite being robust physically. They also don't cycle as deeply as other batteries and are large and heavy for the amount of energy they can store.

The Takeaway

The two most advantageous battery options to consider for your solar solution are lithium-ion batteries and AGM batteries. They are the two most prominent players in the market because they are better suited for off-grid solar systems than the other battery types.

Of course, the capital expenditure on these batteries is constantly changing, but, at present, AGM batteries cost between US$300 and US$500 for a 12V, 200Ah unit. In comparison, lithium-ion batteries with similar ratings will cost between US$1,200 and US$1,500. This clearly shows the advantage of AGM batteries from a cost-saving perspective, but the trade-off comes with the depth of discharge and number of cycles that the batteries are capable of. AGM batteries for this price will typically be able to discharge and charge around 400 times, while lithium-ion batteries can discharge approximately 2,000 times. Although the AGM batteries are a third of the price, the lithium-ion batteries will last five times as long.

Chapter 4:
How To Choose The Right
Solar Panel

Choosing the right solar panel for you may seem a bit daunting, especially in an age where there are more options than we know what to do with. In order to figure out what will work best for you, you need to ask a few questions so you can decide for yourself. There is so much information available online and in the market, so it is helpful to know what to look out for and what to avoid when making your decision. Everyone has an opinion on what's best for you, and worse than that is someone in sales trying to sell a specific product to you. Unfortunately, all salespeople will want to sell a product that they have, so you need to take what they say with a grain of salt. You should be informed of the positives and negatives of any solar panel option, as the salesperson for a specific panel will not give you the negatives that their solar panel has.

Solar panels are all rated according to standard test conditions (STC). This means that all ratings you will find listed on solar panel datasheets for performing and are expected to perform are provided at STC levels. This includes a temperature of 25 degrees Celsius, or 77 degrees Fahrenheit; an altitude at sea level, or less than 1,000m or 3,280 ft; low levels of humidity; and an average amount of solar radiation reaching the earth. Solar radiation intensity determines just how much energy is available at any given location to convert into electricity via the photovoltaic process.

The average used is 1,000 W per square meter. This means that for every square meter of space, or just under 11 square feet, there is 1,000 W of potential power available to convert to electricity using standard PV solar panels, regardless of what type. This is the rating according to direct solar radiation, which is added to via indirect solar radiation. This includes all reflected light off of other surfaces, including pavements and buildings, which increases solar radiation levels by a small amount. This level differs from one location to another depending on the amount of sunlight received in that place.

The amount of solar radiation that is available to you is determined by your geographical location. There are online resources available that indicate the intensity of solar radiation for every place on earth. NASA is to thank for a lot of this data that is available to us. Many locations are fortunate to have a much higher solar radiation available per unit area, and can generate a lot more power with the same number of panels than locations with average solar radiation levels. However, many of these areas also experience high average daily temperatures, which results in the de-rating of the solar panel's ability to generate power. In many instances, these two factors balance out and the benefits of a higher solar radiation intensity don't impact the solar power generation levels of these solar arrays. This means that a desert-mounted solar panel cannot necessarily generate more power than a rooftop installation in France. It's all about associating your solar radiation levels with temperature and where you are in making use of this solar system. If you experience very little direct sunlight, you are likely to draw a much lower level of energy from your solar panels than people living in high solar radiation areas.

Solar panels will generate the most amount of electricity when they are directly facing the sun. This essentially maximizes the surface area of the panels that can be exposed to photons. This means that when you install your solar panels, it is beneficial to have them exposed to the most amount of sunlight throughout the day. Apart from shadows and other potential obstructions that could reduce the amount of sunlight received by the panels, the angle at which you mount them is crucial. This is determined by what is known as the azimuth. The azimuth describes the angle at which the sun rises and sets on the east to west path. Your latitude will change the sun's angle in the sky, and you will want to tilt your panels to face the sun at the highest rate possible. This means that, in the northern hemispheres, such as in the US, your angles will be tilted to face more towards the south rather than lying flat. The opposite is experienced for locations in the southern hemisphere. The general rule of thumb is to take your coordinates, more specifically your latitude, and add 15 degrees for summer and subtract 15 degrees for winter. This is for situations where you intend to adjust the tilt angle of your solar panels from season to season. This action will not affect your energy generation capacity by more than 5%; therefore, many people opt to mount their solar systems at the same latitude angle on a rigid mounting structure and do not adjust between seasons (De Rooij, 2020).

The key is to narrow down your selection so that you know what makes sense and what doesn't. If you want to install a permanent installation on the roof of your home, then your requirements will vary from if you want to put up a few panels on an RV to power you as you take a road trip.

The first thing that you need to ask yourself is what your application will be. Will you have a fixed solar installation in the same set location, such as on the roof of your home, or a mobile solar system on a car, boat, RV, or camping trailer. Think of this as a mobile or non-mobile solution moving forward. The mobile solution needs to be durable and robust enough to handle vibration and other mechanical shocks without being damaged. Non-mobile solutions do not need to be as resilient to vibration, but will need to be strong enough to handle various weather conditions, such as hail storms, without being damaged.

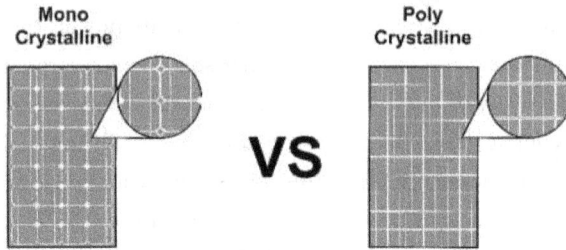

Mono Crystalline **VS** Poly Crystalline

There are two predominant divisions of solar panels available on the market today. They are monocrystalline and polycrystalline. The difference between these two options is in their manufacturing. Monocrystalline solar cells are manufactured from a single silicon crystal, whereas polycrystalline panels are manufactured from several silicon crystals combined. This means that monocrystalline panels are much more expensive because they require a lot more manufacturing finesse in order to keep them uniform. This leads to them being more energy-efficient but a lot more expensive. Over 90% of the solar panels installed today are polycrystalline because they are around 80% as efficient in capturing energy, but they are far cheaper. A typical monocrystalline solar panel will have an energy capturing capacity of around 25%, making them the most efficient solar panel per unit area. They are mostly used in installations where space is limited, but the price isn't a concern. In comparison, a polycrystalline solar panel will have a typical efficiency of 20%, making them substantially less efficient but far cheaper. This level of efficiency may sound extremely low, but that is the amount of energy captured from the sun per unit area, and that number is growing as the materials and technology we apply improve over time.

Rigid and Flexible Solar Panels

Rigid Solar Panels with adjustable mount

Flexible Solar Panel installed on car roof

There are also flexible and rigid solar panel options. Rigid solar panels are designed to be installed as they are on rooftops or mounted in such a way that their bulky structure is not intrusive. Flexible solar panels are designed to be lightweight and compact so that they can streamline a design. This is why flexible solar panels are used in cars and boats more often than in other applications. Once again, they make up a very small market segment because they are considerably more costly. They are also more susceptible to damage from impact, whereas rigid solar panels are designed to be more robust.

Let's take a look at a rooftop installation on an RV as an example to weigh the pros and cons of using a rigid or flexible solar solution. The immediate and obvious advantage of using flexible solar panels over rigid ones in this installation is that they are much lighter and won't weigh the vehicle down. Another massive advantage is that they don't require a bulky frame to mount the panels on and have much less impact on the vehicle's fuel efficiency, as they don't all have a lot of drag. In comparison, rigid solar panels mounted on the roof require a mounting structure and are large panels themselves. These factors combined mean that there will be a lot more drag on the vehicle when driven, and the additional weight will further degrade fuel efficiency. Rigid panels are typically four to five times heavier than flexible panels.

The advantage of rigid solar panels is that they can be moved or adjusted in order to be directed towards the sun, maximizing the power generated. Flexible panels are typically mounted flush to the surface of a vehicle, which means that you cannot adjust the angle of the panels to face the sun directly. Fortunately, there is a technology that is present for flexible solar panels. This is basically raised dots on the panel to improve the solar capturing capability of the panels. However, this is still less effective than simply aiming the panel to face the sun directly, which is more practical than the rigid panels.

The rigid solar panels are very durable, so they are more resistant to scratches to the panels from things like branches. This means that flexible panels are more likely to get damaged in this way than rigid solar panels. The option you pick is purely based on your requirement and budget, as both of these panel types are tried and tested in multiple industries.

In terms of permanently installed panels that will not be moved, such as on houses or panels that are moved to a location and positioned, such as camping trailers, the energy generated per unit area is critical. Many solar panels are 2m long and 1m wide, or roughly 6.5 ft long and 3.5 ft wide, with varying energy generation capabilities. Some of these units will be rated at 250 W, and others at 400 W. It is beneficial to use panels that have a higher energy density, which means that they can generate more power per unit area. These panels are made up of higher efficiency cells, or energy cells that are packed more tightly on a solar panel and hence can generate more power per unit area (Matasci, 2019).

Every solar panel is made up of a string of solar cells that are connected together. Because these cells are typically connected together in series, they all need to be operational for the solar panel to generate power. If there is an open circuit between cells, then the panel will not generate electricity. Many panels have built-in components to try and minimize this risk and still generate some power even if there is damage to one of the cells. For this same reason, solar panels will lose power generated when there is shading. It only takes one cell out of dozens, of which there are typically 72 but can be as high as 96, being in a shadow to reduce the power generated by the entire solar panel. This is because less current is permitted to flow in the entire panel, which can drop the power output by as much as 60%. It is a huge issue to have shading on your solar panel if even a tiny portion of the panel can result in such a huge loss in power generation. Again, there are technologies available to reduce the impact of partial shading on solar panels, but this comes with additional cost. Many solar panels have built-in diodes and other devices which manage power loss far better than standard solar panels. If you run the risk of your solar panels being partly shaded regularly, such as from trees around the solar system, it is worth looking into these types of solar panels.

Always be sure to look out for brands that are internationally accredited. There is no use in bargaining on a solar panel that seems to be of a price that is too good to be true. Suppose the main brands that you recognize, such as CanadaSolar, Jinko, or Trina, are far more expensive than another brand. In that case, it is likely a scam or a product that hasn't met international standards. As with all things in technology, inferior products will not last long, and you will end up wasting your money and have to upgrade later to the units with a standard price.

The most common symbols to look out for on a product to ensure it meets international safety or quality standards are the CE or UL marks. The CE mark stands for "Conformitè

Européenne," European body that confirms that a product meets the body's requirements in terms of safety and quality. Products manufactured or distributed in Europe have to have this marking to represent the quality. In the USA, however, these markings are not compulsory for products being distributed. Many manufacturers still opt to put these symbols on their products to sell their products as good quality products. The UL symbol stands for "Underwriters Laboratories," which indicates that Underwriters Laboratories has inspected samples of the product. They have determined that it conforms to their safety standards. When you are looking for panels to purchase for your solar system, always look for these symbols. Stick to the products that show these labels to know that you are getting a product that has been scrutinized and was found to be safe.

When selecting a solar panel type, you will need to look at what is readily available from solar panel suppliers where you plan to purchase the panels. There are often shortages of a specific size due to large projects buying up all of the availability of certain panels. There are multiple brands that you can choose from, and you will often find that a large order has been placed which hasn't been fully collected, or an excess of panels was ordered for a large client. This could lead to excellent deals and discounted costs on certain panel types. At this stage, it's important for you to look at whether the availability and cost of panels on the market matches the design that you have put together for your solar system. If you specified polycrystalline, 360 W panels, but there is an excellent price for polycrystalline, 320 W panels, then it may be worthwhile to go for the cheaper option, even if you do lose out on some of the power output from each panel. Go back to your original design and see whether this change in panel selection will have an impact, especially if you have to purchase more panels than you had initially intended.

Electrical systems also tend to have a rating that decreases when you go above an altitude of 1,000 m, or 3,280 ft, above sea level. This may impact your installation if you plan to install or make use of it above this level. The same goes for temperature and humidity. Solar panels have a derating above 25 degrees Celsius or 77 degrees Fahrenheit. The depreciation is linear up until approximately 75 degrees Celsius or 167 degrees Fahrenheit. Suppose you experience high temperatures during the summer months. In that case, you may experience a derating factor and only end up generating 90% of the possible power output of the solar panels themselves. It is crucial to consult the specific solar panel datasheet that you plan on using in order to see these values and be realistic in specifying your system.

Solar panels also deteriorate over time due to the photovoltaic effect. Typical panels are tagged with a lifespan of 25 years, and, at that point, they will only be able to generate 40% of the power they were originally rated for. This deterioration is also approximately linear over time, so even after ten years of operation, your panels will only generate around 80% of the power they were in year one. A solar system is a long-term investment, so having this information is important when looking far into the future at the benefits that come from making use of them. It's not to say that after 25 years the solar panels will not continue working for many years after that. It is more relevant to power generation plants that use tens of thousands of solar panels. This loss of possible revenue makes the solar plant non-profitable after 25 years if the panels aren't completely replaced. You could still have a solar system on your house working after 40 years.

This rating is also a conservative average that manufacturers specify and does not equate to every single panel deteriorating at the same rate. There are many pros to using solar panels, but it requires that you fully understand the current limitations of the products in the market today.

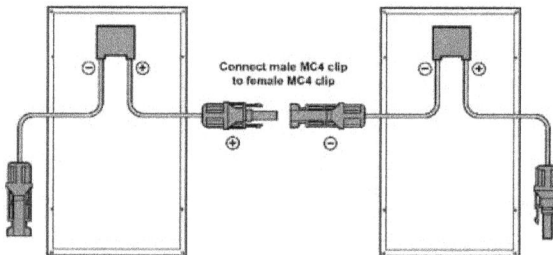

When connecting solar panels to form a string, you will need connecting wires and clips, most commonly the MC4 clips, which have a male and female connection and clip tightly when pushed together. Most solar panels are manufactured to have short lengths of wires, with one wire connected with a male clip and another with a female clip. This makes it easier to discern between the positive and negative terminals. It is essential to connect the positive of one panel into the negative of the adjacent unit and form a string. If you connect a panel the wrong way around, then the voltages will cancel out, and it could damage the internal cells of the solar panel. Fortunately, most units have built-in diodes, which are electronic components that only allow current to flow in one direction and not the other. These diodes prevent current from flowing through one panel, keeping it from running through the entire string of panels.

When you are specifying a solar panel for your application, confirm that the solar panel has these wire leads with the MC4 clips on them. Also, make sure that the leads are long enough to reach between two panels that are mounted right next to each other. Older solar panel models were often supplied with a terminal box with a positive and negative connection point without these cable lengths, meaning that more materials would need to be purchased, and installing the units becomes more labor-intensive. There is no point in saving cost on your solar panels by selecting units without wire leads, known as tails, and ending up spending more when combining the cost of the wires, clips, and solar panels than a more expensive solar panel that comes with these components included.

The same goes for mounting clips. Something as small as having pre-drilled holes for mounting brackets to be used to secure your solar panels can save you time and expendable parts, such as drill bits. Modern solar panels come with an aluminum frame built around the cells. These frames typically have a lip, which means that they can be clamped to a structure and no drilling will be required for the solar panel itself. This maintains its integrity and reduces the risk of accidentally drilling through the protective glass and creating a weak spot in it. Be sure to look for solar panels with this frame if you have selected to use rigid solar panels.

Chapter 5:
How To Choose The Right Wires, Fuses, and Inverter

Now that we have sized the solar system that you require, determined which batteries will suit your application, and established which solar panels will be the best fit, it's time to look at all the other major components you will require for your solar system. This chapter will focus on sizing and selecting your inverter, fuses for protection, and cables to connect the panels, inverter, battery, and loads. It will then expand this to typical mounting structures that are used for various applications. In Chapter 6, the process of installing and testing your solar system will be covered, so the mounting structures presented in this chapter are just to help you select the right units for your requirements.

Sizing Your Cables and Wires

To start, the cables that you use have a significant impact on your solar system. There are specific single-core cables that are required to use for DC systems. Cables rated to handle 1,000 V of AC power aren't necessarily suited to use in DC circuits. When looking at cable options, make sure that you select one with a DC-rated voltage and ensure that the string of solar panels you have to connect to your inverter does not exceed this DC voltage. The current rating of the cable that you require is also extremely important. If you have a string of panels that will supply 10 A, then the cable you select needs to be rated at 10 A or higher. It is advisable to select a cable that is one size larger than the rated current that you require. This is to ensure that they can handle a short circuit current. Fortunately, with solar systems, the fault current is very close to the full load current of the solar panels. This is because they cannot supply excess power to a short circuit, unlike many other sources, such as generators.

Another consideration that you need to look at is the length of the cables from the solar panels to your inverter. The longer a cable is, the more internal resistance they have and the more power losses you will experience. There is a phenomenon known as voltage drop on cables due to length. Most solar systems are designed to have the inverter close to the panels, so your cable length shouldn't be long enough to create a voltage drop across them. When selecting an AC cable to be installed on the output of your inverter to a distribution board, this may be a consideration that you have to look at. We will cover this once we complete the requirements to consider in your DC cables.

When considering the type of cable you require, it's essential to think about the nature of the installation. Some cables are manufactured with protective armoring, which is useful for cables buried in the ground or mounted where they could experience an impact that risks cutting into the cable. The downside of an armored cable is that it is more expensive and more rigid. It's far easier to bend an unarmoured cable, making it easier to install. A word of caution here: All cables have a minimum bending radius. This means that if you need to bend a 90 degree angle in the cable, you have to bend it in a curve rather than put a 90 degree bend on the cable, as this will damage it and create a weak spot. All cables have this bending radius listed on a datasheet for reference. It's usually given in inches or millimeters and assists you in installing the cables according to the manufacturer's specifications.

Another consideration is in using cables that are resistant to ultraviolet (UV) light. The sun gives off UV light, and this can degrade cables over time. Cables that are not resistant to UV light will become hard and crack. If a crack goes from the outer cable to the live conductor inside, then you may experience a fault or risk being electrocuted if you touch this part of the cable. As all solar panels need to be mounted outdoors in order to capture the sunlight, selecting UV-resistant cables is recommended.

Most solar panels are manufactured with lengths of positive and negative cables with connector clips on them. These cable lengths are known as tails, and the cables that you select should connect to these tails. A lot of the time, solar panels have tails that are long enough to connect panels to either side of it to form the strings, and you only need to connect to the first and last panel in a string to connect it to the inverter. This saves cost on cables and connector clips. You will need to make sure that the cable you select will be able to fit the right connector clip on it to connect to the solar panel clips. These clips have a range of wire sizes that will fit them and are designed to fit into all the common cable sizes typically used in solar installations.

A typical cable that you could select would be a 2.5mm2, single-core, unarmoured, 1,000 voltage in direct current (VDC), UV resistant cable. Many datasheets are available from different cable manufacturers, including Aberdare and Lapp, among other known brand names. When it comes to your AC cable connecting from your inverter to a distribution board, the ratings you need to consider are very similar. The main difference is that AC has inductance as well as resistance, which combine to form impedance. Impedance is the same as resistance in a DC system, which is what restricts the flow of current and creates losses. It is similar to how drag creates air resistance that reduces the ability of vehicles to travel fast. Essentially, there are additional losses to consider with AC cables that aren't present in DC systems. Fortunately, these tend to be small, and you won't need to concern yourself with short cable runs.

How to Earth or Ground Your System

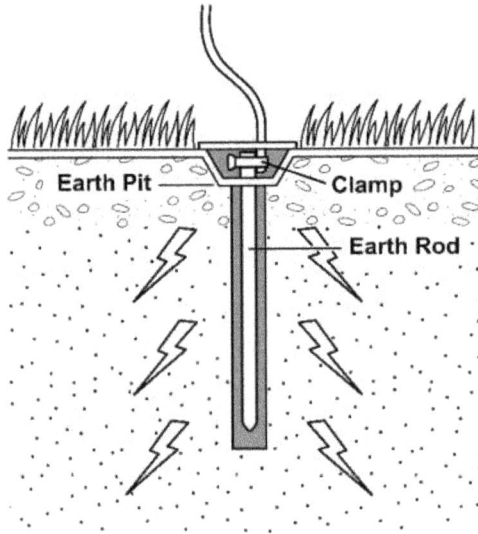

Another major consideration that many people neglect to address is the earthing of your solar system. Earthing, or grounding, refers to linking parts of your solar system to earth, making it safe. When it comes to earthing, one of the most important aspects to consider is known as equipotential. This means that different points have the same connection to the earth; therefore, no potential difference can exist between them, resulting in current flowing from one point to another, especially through a person. It is a critical safety feature that all electrical installations need to consider.

Picture a moment when you have touched something conductive, be it a door handle or car body, and you received a static shock. The reason for this small shock is that you have a different potential difference from the object that you touch. Many times, this is caused due to shoes that you wear which insulate you from the ground. This, combined with touching or rubbing various things, results in a buildup of charge of one type or another. The surfaces that you touch moments before a static shock are almost always neutral, at an equipotential charge as the earth.

You, however, have a built-up positive or negative charge which will dissipate when you come in contact with the earth, resulting in a static shock. The purpose of equipotential earthing is to ensure that all non-live parts of an electrical system are at the same potential as earth, making them safe to touch one another. The other purpose of having equipotential earthing is that any earth fault will be detected and isolated. An earth fault means that a conductor carrying electricity has a connection to a component that should not be conducting electricity. If you have a toaster constricted by metal, then the last thing you want is for the entire toaster to become live and electrocute you if you touch it. Without equipotential earthing, you would not even realize that the toaster's body was live. With equipotential earthing and the correct earthing protection, as soon as a live wire touches the toaster's body from within, the equipotential bonding conductor leads that power to earth, resulting in a trip and isolation of electricity flowing to the toaster.

More than half of the faults that occur in electrical systems are due to earth faults or incorrect earthing, so it is a good starting point.

CONSIDERATION FOR LIGHTNING RISKS

Another major aspect of solar systems that you should consider is lightning protection. Lightning behaves in much the same way that static electricity behaves. There is a build up of charge between the clouds and the earth, resulting in a voltage that spirals until lightning results in a burst of current from one to the other, discharging the buildup of charge. The trouble with solar systems is that they act as a beacon for lightning. The myth that lightning strikes the highest point has some validity to it, but probably not in the way that you perceive it.

When you install your solar system, you should carry out a lightning risk assessment to know what type of protection you should install. The last thing you want is for your solar panels to be hit with a lightning strike, causing your solar system to need replacement. A typical lightning risk assessment uses the rolling sphere method to determine all the at-risk points of a lightning strike. At the end of the day, lightning is trying to reach equipotential earth. If there is an array of solar panels, then there are many areas where lightning may strike. This is where you need to install an equipotential lightning rod with its own dedicated link to earth. These lightning rods are not necessarily the massive poles that you see atop skyscrapers, but are relatively short lightning rods that are able to reduce the risk of lightning striking any one of the adjacent panels using the rolling sphere method.

Historically, lightning masts were specified according to a general rule. From the tip of the lightning rod, if you took a 45-degree angle down towards earth in all directions and drew an imaginary line down, that is the level of protection that it can offer. For example, if you had a 10 foot high lightning rod, it could only effectively protect against lightning strikes in a 10 foot radius around the rod. This method is still a good rule of thumb, but the improved method is known as the rolling sphere method. In this method, an imaginary sphere of a diameter determined by the level of protection required is rolled over your installation, and any point that it touches should be fitted with a lightning rod of a specific height. It sounds confusing, but imagine you have a beach ball and you roll it over a kitchen counter. Each point that it touches requires a lightning rod. Now imagine that a lightning rod is a mug placed where the ball first touches the counter. The beach ball now needs to roll over the mug. When the ball touches the counter again, you need another mug or lightning rod, and so on. By the end of rolling the beach ball over the counter, the mugs should prevent the ball from touching the counter altogether. This is like having lightning rods placed on a solar array. Instead of the lightning reaching your solar panels, like the beach ball not reaching the countertop, the lighting will strike the lightning rods, like the beach ball only touching the mugs.

The goal with solar systems is to have fewer lightning rods of lower height to reduce any impact from potential shading or obstructions due to having these rods stick out from your solar system. It is a cheap exercise to add these lightning arrestors, and they may well protect your panels, cables, inverter, and batteries from a catastrophic failure due to a lightning strike. Also, many insurance companies will insist that you have some form of lightning protection in order to cover your solar system or what your solar system is mounted on, such as a house. Insurance companies recognize the fire hazard that comes with a solar system, and you don't want to lose everything without any coverage.

All solar systems, especially those installed on houses, require an easily accessible kill switch. This is typically connected and mounted outside the vehicle or house so that, if there is a fire, flood, or another emergency, the solar system can be isolated from the outside without anyone having to risk their lives to go inside and risk electrocution or worse.

SPECIFYING YOUR INVERTER AND CHARGE CONTROLLER

When it comes to the inverter that you select, the main criteria you need to consider is the power capacity of the inverter. If you determine that you will require 3 kW of power at any given time, you need to have an inverter to meet this demand. It is recommended that you select an inverter that is oversized for your current requirements in case you expand or need to add more load at a later stage. It is also important to figure out how many strings of solar panels can connect to your inverter. Some inverters may be rated for just a single string, while others will cater for two or three strings. This is also relevant to the system voltage of your solar system. Each panel that you add to your string will increase the DC voltage of the string. Inverters will have a maximum DC voltage rating for their input, and you cannot exceed this voltage. It would also be a waste not to make use of voltage to maximize your power generation capability. Inverters are rated with a specific power availability, and this requires both a voltage of a certain range and a current of a certain range. The best practice is to maximize your voltage as far as possible in order to get the power that you require. If the rated string voltage of an inverter is 120 Volts of DC power, then connecting a string rated at 48 Volts DC would reduce the power capability of the inverter. It is possible to expand in the future for such a consideration. Still, it would also be possible to expand the system by connecting a second string of panels in parallel to the first string that has been connected. This is typically determined by the configuration and connection of your combiner box or the rating of and number of DC inputs on your inverter.

Inverters also put out a high-pitched sound that, in some cases, falls into the audible range for humans. It's important to consult the inverter manual or, preferably, see a demo unit in action to avoid purchasing an inverter that gives off this noise, as it can be highly annoying and result in headaches over time. Most inverters will have an operational frequency rating that you can look at and compare to audible frequencies, which typically range from 20 Hertz to 20,000 Hertz for people with perfect hearing. Do not confuse this audible frequency range with the switching frequency of the semiconductive devices.

One of the most useful features of many modern-day off-grid inverters is that they are equipped with a charge controller built into the unit. This makes it a single device to connect your batteries, solar panels, and AC loads to via a DB. It makes the inverters a space and cost-saver in the long run. The inverter will be able to convert the DC power generated into AC power for your consumption when the sun is out. At the same time, the excess power generated will be used to charge your batteries via the inverter's built-in charge controller. This allows you to maximize the power that your solar panels generate and avoid wasting power. This system is streamlined since there is only one controlling device handling all the functionality. This added efficiency and quick response of the unit make it the most functional connection for inverters. Suppose your load demand is too great for your solar panels to handle. In that case, the charge controller works in the opposite direction and power is drawn from the batteries to make up the difference between the power that you generate and the power demanded by your load. This is expanded into the night when your solar panels are not generating any power, and your batteries are relied on to supply power to your loads. The change between operations is seamless and uninterrupted, so you will not even be aware of the change from solar to battery supply.

When it comes to charge controllers, many people don't understand their purpose. If batteries charge at 12 VDC, and you have a 12 VDC solar panel, why can't you just connect the one directly onto the other? The main reason for this is that batteries are sensitive to either voltage or current. Some batteries require a stable voltage level that doesn't spike too high, which could damage the battery's insulation, such as with gel-type batteries. On the other hand, some batteries cannot be charged quickly from a large current flowing through them, such as with AGM batteries. To avoid these two problems, charge controllers monitor and limit the amount of current that flows to the batteries as well as the voltage exposed to the batteries in order to charge them according to their manufacturer specifications. In this way, your batteries will experience a longer lifespan and will be suitably protected while charging and discharging.

These devices are typically connected to solar panel strings in the DC circuit. The advantage of having a charge controller on the DC circuit is that there are fewer losses than on the AC side, such as battery charger units consisting of a bidirectional rectifier and filter unit. Battery chargers that are connected to the AC circuit are more commonly seen in grid-tied solar systems, as they will charge batteries from the solar power and the grid without discerning between the two.There is no grid with off-grid solar systems; therefore, batteries will only be charged from the solar panels. Additionally, these batteries act as the source of power when the solar panels are not generating power, so if they run out of charge, there is no power at all. This differs from grid-tied systems where the grid can still charge the batteries even if the solar panels cannot.

Solar inverters that have a built-in battery charger system are preferable to using two different devices. A lot of this has to do with the intelligence that is built into modern-day inverters. Most leading brands have what is known as a human-machine interface (HMI) touch screen and a connection to the internet. These devices often have a read-only or adjustable phone application that you can use to connect to your inverter from your phone. The displays are very useful and include total power generated by your solar panels, percentage of charge on your batteries, your load demand at any given time, and trending data for you to track your average power usage and plan better. You will also see if it makes sense to expand your solar array or battery bank based on your needs in this way.

These features are typically available for you no matter where you are, provided you have an internet connection and provided your inverter has the capability and internet connection. It is password-protected, so there is very low risk when it comes to cybersecurity. Most modern systems are equipped with a view-only mode, which allows you to see all of the settings and live data but not change anything. This secures you from someone logging into your system and reducing the efficiency or changing settings that don't work best for you. We live in the age of information, and the more data you are able to gather and observe, the easier it is to monitor, repair, or carry out maintenance on your system. If you note that the power generated by your solar panels is lower this month than the previous one, then perhaps you should clean your panels and see what impact this will have. It's also a key indicator as to how well your batteries are aging. Inverters equipped with battery charge controllers will also have basic monitoring functionality to inform you if there is a problem with your batteries. This allows you to replace or repair a battery before it fails or reaches its end of life, leaving you in a blackout situation.

SPECIFYING YOUR FUSES

Another feature included in your inverter that you should look out for is having built-in fuses and surge arrestors. These devices can be installed separately and are just as effective, but it saves cost to already have these devices sized and installed internally in your inverter. Also, make sure the inverter is lightweight and easy to install. Most inverters will come with a wall mount kit that allows you to drill and mount the inverter into a wall easily. Make sure that you select the right mounting kit based on the wall type. Metal, wood, and concrete will all have slightly different mounting kits based on materials best suited to keep the inverter sturdy.

If your selected inverter is not equipped with built-in fuses, then you will have to specify and purchase them yourself. It's important to identify the areas where fuses will be most practical. If you have a distribution board on the AC side of your inverter, then all protection devices should be mounted in there. This means that you need to worry about fuses coming into your inverter from your solar panels. These fuses need to be mounted somewhere, and typically what people will do when installing fuses is to use a combiner box. A combiner box links all your strings of panels together and has fuses and surge arrestors built into it. Your solar panel string lengths and panel sizes need to be considered when specifying your fuses. The more panels you have in series, the more current will be drawn from the solar array. This is also relevant because the rated total load current of solar panels, typically at 25 degrees Celsius, or 77 degrees Fahrenheit, is less than 10% different from the solar panel fault current. Essentially, the fuse sizes have to be very precise in order to avoid blowing a fuse when the solar array is operating correctly and not having a fuse blow when there is a legitimate short circuit fault. Additionally, not all fuses are suitable to use in DC circuits, so you need to specify that the fuses will be used in a DC system and what the expected voltage will be. Fuses are typically rated for 1,000 VAC, but this would only be suitable for use in DC systems of just over 700 VDC. This is why caution is needed when choosing your solar system fuses. Suppose you have a single string of panels. In that case, you only need to refer to the maximum operating current and fault current of a single panel in order to specify your fuses for a string connected in series. If the full rated current is 9

A and the fault current is rated at 11 A, then you should ideally choose a 10 A fuse in order to protect your string from short circuits (Clifton, 2016).

CHAPTER 6:
BUILD YOUR OWN SOLAR POWER SYSTEM

The process of taking the theory covered in the above chapters and putting it into a physical installation requires some fundamentals that are necessary to consider. This chapter will look at practical ways to purchase the right equipment, install it correctly, and prove the system works the way you designed it. As with all designs, it is always good to test the system in a simulation before you buy so you don't find that it isn't correct or as effective as you had anticipated after going out and spending the money. There are many online resources that are free of charge, and we recommend Helioscope. It is a paid software, but there is a 30 day free trial that you can make use of. In the software, you can mimic how your solar panels will be installed, specify the exact inverter and battery backup, and the software will determine how much energy you will be able to capture over the year and pick up if there is something that you have specified which simply won't work. It's safe to say that the energy output from solar panels varies from summer to winter. Surprisingly, solar panels often perform better in the winter months because many places are drier and do not experience as much rainfall or snowfall during the winter. This increases the amount of daylight sun hours per day, increasing the quantity of energy generated by the solar panels. Another point is that solar panels have a higher efficiency when kept in cooler conditions with high levels of sunlight. They typically perform best at around 20 degrees Celsius or 68 degrees Fahrenheit, but it can vary. Temperatures above 25 degrees Celsius or 77 degrees Fahrenheit result in a degradation of energy efficiency (Almerini, 2021). Because of this phenomenon, winter months often lead to more efficient solar power generation.

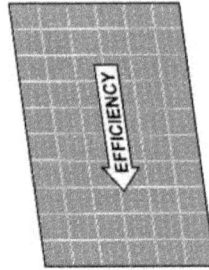

20° C or 68° F   Above 25° C or 77° F

However, due to the reduced number of hours of sun in the sky during the day, you will likely see a drop in daylight sun hours and energy produced throughout the day. Moreover, most users have higher energy requirements in the winter months than they do in the summer months due to additional lighting and, potentially, heating devices that are used in winter. It's important to know your winter and summer power demands so that you don't size your system for one season but neglect the other. This may not be relevant to you if you are installing a solar system on a holiday home or RV, which you only make use of in the summer, but it is still an important consideration when sizing your solar system. Software such as Helioscope is user-friendly and takes you through a step-by-step guide to size your system according to the theory you have learned and highlights areas you may have missed along the way. It will automatically consider your geographical location, predict meteorological data based on historical data, and help you see what you can expect to get out of your solar system.

Building on this note, one of the first things you need to decide when installing your solar panels is to angle them to capture the most energy from the sun. The angle of the sun shifts between winter and summer. If you live in the northern hemisphere, the sun will not rise due east and set due west. Instead, it rises and sets further south, and how far south is dependent on the seasons. The sun will rise and set further south during the winter compared to the summer, which can have a massive impact on how much power you can generate. The thing to consider here is how much you should tilt your solar panels towards the south in order to capture the most sunlight possible. Of course, this is reversed in the southern hemisphere, where the sun rises and sets to the north.

It's a good idea to measure the space where you want to install your panels before you go out and purchase them. Measuring the space also involves verifying the areas that will receive sunlight throughout the day and which areas may experience shade. Consider this with the different times of the year, as a shadow may not be cast during the summer months on a certain area, but is cast in the same area during winter. It's also a good idea to decide where you wish to install your inverter, battery charger, and batteries. This will help you determine the cable route that you will take when installing your DC cables from your solar panels to your inverter. Also, consider where your existing AC DB is located if this is relevant to your installation.

If you are installing your panels on the roof of a house, what type of roofing is it? Corrugated iron and tiles require different mounting clips to secure the panels to a rigid structure, such as the roof. Also, consider that you will need to clean your solar panels at least once every few months. Installations aren't just about what is convenient for you, but also what is practical in the future, especially regarding maintenance and replacement work that you may have to carry out in the future.

Now is a good time to consider the tools that you will require for installing the solar system. For the most part, the tools are relatively simple. A multimeter of some kind is highly recommended so that you can measure each solar panel as well as voltage, earthing, and frequency in your AC circuit. It's a handy tool while installing and testing your system to prove that it is working how you designed it. You will need standard handheld tools such as screwdrivers, especially a small, flat screwdriver that is commonly called a terminal screwdriver. This tool is typically used for terminating wires in electrical installations. A socket set, spanners and Allen wrenches are useful to have, as many inverters and mounting structures will require that you have these tools.

You will also require wire cutters or side cutters in order to cut cables or wires where needed. If you are using a larger cable with armoring, you may require a knife such as a Stanley knife to cut through the cable's outer sheath before stripping the armoring. It is useful to have a long nose and standard pliers for this purpose as well. Wire strippers are useful to strip the insulation off the ends of wires off to mount a connector clip, lug, or bootlace in order to connect the wire to a terminal of some kind. If you do not have wire strippers, it is possible to strip wires with side cutters or wire cutters.

The next tool is essential for electrical installations, and that is a crimping tool. This tool is used to crimp the wire with a lug, bootlace, or connector clip. In almost all electrical installations, these terminations are used instead of using bare copper or aluminum.

Crimping MC4 Connectors

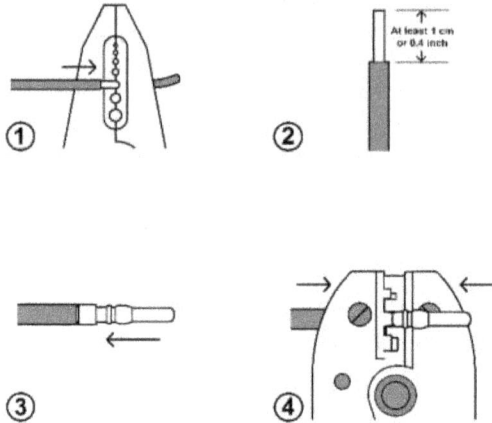

There may be an additional need to have some power tools handy. It is ideal to use battery-powered tools, as they are more practical with installations such as solar systems. A battery-powered drill and angle grinder should be suitable to cater to all of your power tool needs.

The method for installing your solar panels is quite straightforward once you can identify the surface you are installing. A rooftop mounted solar system will vary from a ground-mounted system or a flush-mounted system on an RV or boat. Some cabins do not have a tilt angle that benefits from angling it towards the sun. In order to mount the panels so that they can capture as much power from sun up to sundown, it may be more practical to build a mounting structure to maximize the panels' alignment with the sun, which involves using, preferably, an aluminum frame.

Something that many people neglect to do when it comes to installing their solar system or carrying out any project that requires you to do it yourself is to choose and learn how to use your tools correctly. It may seem very straightforward to crimp a lug onto a wire using a wire crimping tool, but many people will do it incorrectly. Even electricians often fail to follow best practices when making use of handheld tools. This results in poor workmanship and faults that would have been easily avoided if the installers had used their tools correctly. The more you use your tools, the more using them becomes second nature to you, but the first few times you use a new tool may feel unusual.

This goes for all the simple tools that are required for this installation. When stripping the insulation material off of wires using wire strippers or side cutters, be sure to strip off the right amount for the lug, clip, or bootlace that you intend to fasten onto the wire. Lugs require a short section of approximately 1 cm, or 0.4 inches, of the conductor (typically copper) to be exposed on your wire. Next up is to put the lug over the wire with the clamp section over the live conductor and the insulated section over the wire's insulation. You also need to make sure that you crimp the lug on the right way around. When a lug is crimped, there should be no copper or live conductor strands sticking out on the live connection part of the lug. The insulated part of the lug should also have a snug fit over the wire conductor without any live parts of the wire being exposed here. You can test how well a wire is crimped by pulling on it to confirm that it won't slip off the wire at any point.

This is just an example of how to use one of the handheld tools that many people aren't familiar with. There are many resources, including YouTube or even the supplier of the tools, that you can go to in order to learn good tool work practices. This preparation and learning activity may seem trivial, but it is a useful skill to have for any DIY project moving forward.

All new installations that you make to your home or vehicle are based on international or local standards. There are wiring standards, sizing standards, and aspects that will directly affect your solar installation. There is a good chance that these standards will not directly impact you in going off-grid, but there is a reason that they have been drafted, and you should not ignore them. It encompasses every small detail that you can possibly consider in your system, from the inverter you select, to earthing and safety requirements, to the mechanical reliability of your structures. Building a solar system that adheres to international standards means that you will automatically install a legal, ethical system and fits your requirements as need be.

RV MOUNTED SOLAR SYSTEM

When it comes to RV solar systems, you want to mount your panels straight to the RV roof to reduce any drag you might experience while driving. It is possible to mount a rooftop system that is adjustable once you are parked to absorb more sunlight, but this may not be the best option. It has a higher initial capital cost and means that you have moving components that may require replacing. It also means that you have to get up onto the roof to adjust the angle every time you stop, which isn't a practical option. It also means that you need to ensure that the solar panels are flush and secure when you wish to drive again.

A simpler solution is going with a rooftop mount system that is flexible and does not adjust. You also don't want to drill too many holes in the roof to reduce the risk of leaking. There are great sealants available on the market that prevent leaking, but they are less effective than a system that does not require drilling to mount solar panels. There is the option of using double-sided tape that is highly resilient to environmental conditions and will adequately secure your solar panels to the roof. One such type of double-sided tape is very high bond (VHB) tape. It varies in length and width, but a good option from a reliable manufacturer to use when mounting your panels to the roof would be 3M 4941 VHB tape (Dennis, 2019). This tape is very durable and is very good at maintaining its adhesive properties even with large temperature fluctuations. When applying this tape, the surface that you mount it to must be clean. Making use of alcohol or methylated spirits even after washing the surface clean is a good idea. This will reduce the risk of dust or particles getting caught in the area that you will stick the solar panels to. The disadvantage of using this type of tape over using a drill and mount system is that you will have difficulty removing the panel at a later stage if you wish to remove or replace it.

If this is a concern that you have, then opt for drilling and tapping with a flush mount kit for the solar panels of your choice. You will have to add sealant around each area you have drilled and test that the sealant works effectively. Self-leveling sealant is readily available and will be required for the DC wires to be installed from the solar panels outside the RV to the inverter, batteries, and charge controller system on the inside.

BOAT MOUNTED SOLAR SYSTEM

A boat-mounted system has a lot of similarities to RV-mounted systems. The main thing to consider with a boat-mounted system is that there is a lot of moisture. The panels and outside will almost certainly get wet with saltwater rather than just rainwater (depending on whether you have a freshwater or saltwater application in mind). Corrosion at sea level is notoriously bad, and this factor shouldn't be ignored with your solar system either. Fortunately, solar panels and solar wire connectors (typically MC4 connectors) are rated to handle this type of environment. It is still good practice to clean your solar panels with fresh water frequently, just as you would the rest of the deck on any boat. Soap water and clean freshwater are all that you need.

It's also of note to point out that, in a boat installation, there is a lot of movement on deck, and the movement of a boat results in a lot more impact style motion compared to driving on the road in an RV installation. This could result in areas that have been sealed being weakened or cracked over time, which could lead to a leak from the exterior to the interior of the hull. In order to prevent this from occurring, you should use high-quality sealant that is rated for marine applications. These are readily available from hardware stores, and this is an area where you shouldn't worry about cost-saving and should focus on purchasing a high-quality product. It's also advisable that you buy excess sealant to have on hand in the future in case you have any issues with leaking due to natural wear and tear.

Small Home or Cabin Mounted Solar System

This type of installation is almost always going to be made up of rigid solar panels. The system is non-mobile; therefore, the weight and air resistance would not be as much of a factor as with RV's, boats, and other mobile solar systems. A word of caution here is to confirm that you will not compromise the integrity of the existing structure where you mount the panels. Whether big or small, all cabins and houses are designed to carry a certain weight on them. This usually takes into consideration various roofing tiles and extreme weather conditions that exert additional force on them. They also cater to water or snow build-up, and even the weight of a person walking over them. Now, add the weight of a dozen or so solar panels, each weighing around 20 kilograms, or 44 pounds, then add frames, wires, lightning rods, and all additional support brackets that may be required. This could add as much as 300 kilograms, or 660 pounds, of additional weight on top of your roof, which is a large additional weight. The last thing that you want is to have your roof collapse when you go up to clean your panels or have the panels act as a sail in the event of high wind, ripping them off of your roof.

Washing Roof Mounted PV Panels

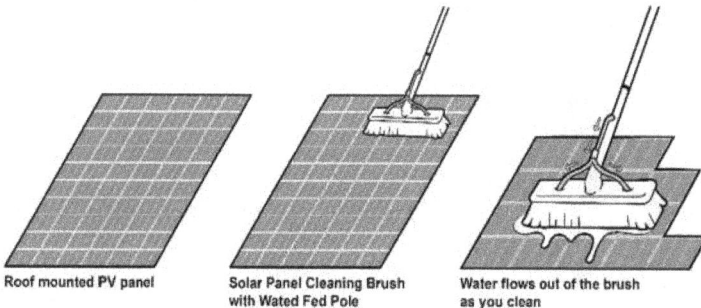

Roof mounted PV panel | Solar Panel Cleaning Brush with Wated Fed Pole | Water flows out of the brush as you clean

It's also important to consider your access to running water, particularly with enough pressure to clean solar panels mounted on top of the roof of a structure. Running water is ideal to use in order to clean your panels. You also need to consider having a ladder to easily gain access to the panels in order to clean them. Additionally, mounting the panels on top of roof tiling or corrugated iron requires mounting, which may compromise the waterproofing of your roof. Be sure to test that you have adequately sealed the roof after you have mounted the panels before experiencing rainfall. Take care when determining your cable route when taking the DC wires from the solar panel strings to the location in your home where you have decided to mount the solar inverter, preferably close to the DB. The shorter your cable length is, the fewer losses you will experience, and the less cable you will have to purchase. This doesn't mean that you should run a direct line from one point to another, as there may be obstacles in the way. You want your cable runs to be neat and not to take away from the aesthetic of your home. You may want to install the cables in skirting or cable trunking. You can run the wires above the ceiling, then drill through the ceiling and run the wires down to the inverter. In this way, you will only have to worry about sealing this point in the roof down to the inverter. It will also avoid having the eyesore of wires running through your living space.

Cable Management Using Cable Ties

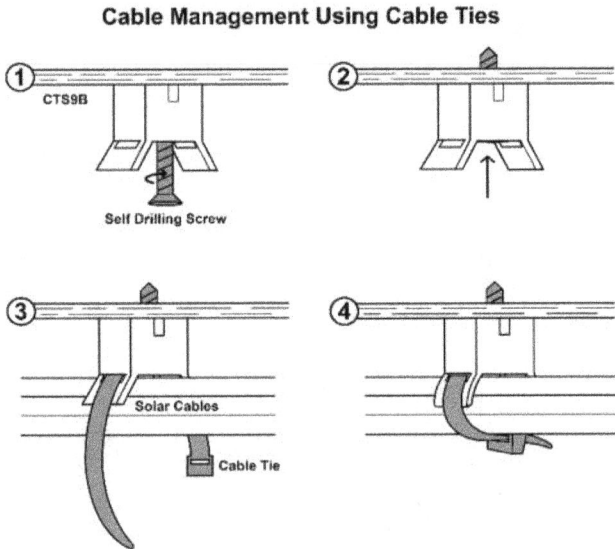

Don't forget to keep vermin out of the areas where electrical wires will be located. Rats and other rodents are nasty with this, as they will eat their way through the insulation of your wiring and cause a short circuit and loss of ability to generate power. Make use of flame retardant foam where necessary to keep vermin out and remove the fire hazard that comes with using regular sealant spray foam.

Solar systems on any home can drive up the property value substantially. However, this does also come with additional expenses when it comes to home insurance policies. These premiums will inevitably go up due to the addition of a solar system on the roof. It may also impact your property tax rates, depending on the country, state, or county you live in.

CONNECTION METHODS

The most common method of connecting your solar system is to have your solar panels and batteries connected to your charge controller. A typical charge controller and inverter will have connection diagrams that the manufacturer provides. There will generally be more than one option, but there will always be a recommended setup that matches your requirement.

The most common connection between the primary components is having a common negative terminal between the battery charger, solar panels, and batteries. In DC circuits, you always want to have the same reference voltage. In many installations, this negative terminal of a DC circuit is earthed, such as in cars. However, in solar systems, it is highly recommended that the negatives are not earthed. There are circumstances where this is required, but a good rule of thumb is to leave the negative terminal floating unless the manufacturer explicitly recommends that you earth them. The term "floating" is used to describe a point that may be earthed but is intentionally left without an earth reference point.

The inverter will have a positive and negative input from the batteries as well as a bypass connection from the charge controller, typically on the positive input. The charge controller controls this bypass connection. When the batteries are fully charged, excess power is bypassed from the batteries and connected directly to the inverter.

The inverter will then have a connection on the AC side to your load via a DB. This connection is via an AC cable. There is typically an isolation and protection device in the DB that acts as an incomer. The solar panel power is an incoming power to be distributed to where you require it.

Some inverters directly input from the batteries with a built-in charge controller and a direct connection to the solar panels. These units typically have no maximum power point tracker (MPPT) connections or a built-in MPPT connection. Other solar inverters have input from solar panels via an external MPPT. An MPPT is essentially a converter device that optimizes the balance between the DC voltage of the solar panels, your battery bank, and your AC system. It is beneficial to have more than one MPPT device built into your solar inverter or housed externally. Two separate units can monitor and optimize the power generated by solar panels oriented in different ways without incurring losses across your whole solar array.

When you hook your battery system up, you need to refer to the voltage rating of the charge controller and solar inverter battery input. Many of the products available on the market are limited to 12 V or 24 V, so connecting your batteries in a 48 V configuration is not a viable option. Suppose you were to connect a series of batteries resulting in a 48 V configuration to an MPPT or inverter input that is only rated for 24 V. In that case, you will damage the insulation and other electronics inside the device. Fortunately, most devices have built-in over-voltage protection, which will blow in a similar way to a fuse if the voltage level exceeds the rated voltage. These components, known as metal oxide varistors (MOVs), will have to be replaced if they are damaged in this way, and your device will not be able to operate until this is done.

You have two options when connecting multiple batteries: Connect them in either a series or parallel configuration. If you connect them in series, their voltage will increase, whereas when you connect them in parallel, their voltage will remain the same. The power goes up with the same proportions in both cases. In the case of a parallel connection, the current, or amps, supplied doubles instead of the voltage. It is always recommended that you use an even number of batteries and match your connections throughout. If you want to make up a 24 V battery setup, it isn't good practice to use three 12 V batteries. Suppose you were to put two batteries in parallel and connect these two in series with one more battery. In that case, you will be able to achieve your overall 24 V system. Still, the battery alone will have a lot more current flowing through it, which typically leads to heating issues, charging problems, and a reduction in the battery lifespan.

Ensure that the wires you use to connect your batteries are thick enough to handle the current that will flow through them. It is common practice to clamp lugs onto these fairly thick wires and add heat shrink wrap to maintain the insulation and avoid flashovers of any kind. Heat shrink is an insulating material, similar to insulation tape, but it does not use glue or other adhesives that wear over time. The heat shrink wrap is placed over the point where the lug and wire connect, and when heat is applied, the insulation material shrinks to fit snugly over the connection point.

Using Heat Shrinkable Tubes

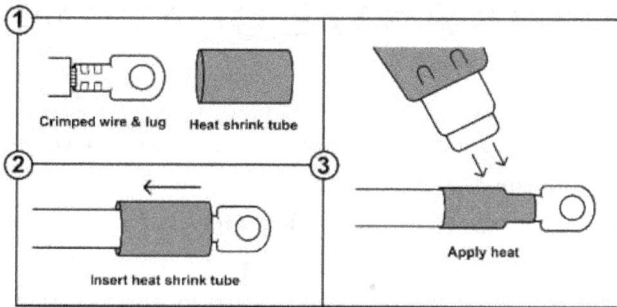

It's also good practice to install a fuse, or DC-rated circuit breaker between your DC devices. This implies that you require a DC circuit breaker or DC-rated fuse in your connections between your battery charge controller and batteries and between your batteries and your inverter battery inputs. The added benefit of having these devices is that they can act as safety isolation devices if you need to do any maintenance or replacement work on your DC system. When working on your batteries, you should turn the circuit breaker off or open the circuit using the circuit breakers between the batteries and charge controller and between the batteries and inverter before you work on them. This will reduce any risk of electrocution or injury from the batteries discharging through you when working on them.

This can be expanded into protection or isolation devices on the output of your inverter. All DBs that feed your loads should have their own protection devices, such as fuses or circuit breakers. Circuit breakers are the preferred method in these installations as they can be reset and used for up to 10,000 operations. In comparison, a fuse will operate once and burn out, requiring replacement. Fuses respond quicker than any other protection device, but a circuit breaker is preferable in the case of small household loads, even though it takes between three and five times as long to trip. Fuses will blow within 20 milliseconds of a major short circuit, whereas circuit breakers will typically trip after around 100 milliseconds. This doesn't add a significant amount of risk for small power systems, such as homes, RV's, and other small-scale solar systems.

Chapter 7:
Blueprints And Equations

In order to fully understand and implement the theory introduced above, you will need some common equations to calculate your requirements. The last thing you want is to undersize your solar system and be left in blackout scenarios on a frequent basis. It's also detrimental to oversize your solar system and end up paying excessive amounts for a system that you don't fully utilize. If your system can handle a house, but you only require it for your RV on weekend getaways, then you may have oversized your system. This is commonly referred to as an overdesign. There is nothing inherently wrong with overdesigning your solar system, only that you will end up paying more for the system than required without reaching a return on investment for the system.

When calculating the size of your solar system, you need to look at the loads that you will supply with it. Now is the time to look at the power or current requirements of the combined loads and determine how often the loads will be connected and how much power they will draw at any given time. If you are supplying three sockets rated for 15 amps, it doesn't mean that you will be using 15 amps 24 hours per day. The two factors that you need to look at are the frequency of using loads and how much of the loads will be used at any given time. With a 15 A socket outlet, you may be using 10 A, so you would be oversizing your solar system to cater for this. In the same way, you could size your backup battery storage to supply these loads for 24 hours of the day only to realize later that a lot of loads will be for things that only draw power for half of the time.

Let's start by looking at how many batteries you require for your needs. We will also consider how many solar panels you require and the type of inverter you require. The best inverters on the market have a battery charger module installed in them, as discussed in Chapter 5. These units typically have more than one MPPT to connect strings of panels angled in different ways to maximize the peak sun hours of different seasons. That being said, you need to know what is required from an inverter as well as its efficiency. Furthermore, there are things that manufacturers and distributors typically wouldn't disclose to an end-user that will be discussed in this chapter. An end-user is the description that manufacturers use to describe a person or company that will use their products. This separates them from distributors or stockholders who sell the products on behalf of the manufacturer. The ratings that manufacturers display on their datasheets are legitimate but are often based on ideal circumstances. In reality, some losses are taken that decrease the efficiency of products, but most manufacturers do not elaborate on this in detail, as it shows the limitations of their product. This is not openly displayed by competitors either.

A typical small home with two bedrooms and two bathrooms will require about eight sockets. Assuming each socket is rated at 5 amperes, there will be a total available capacity of 40 amps. That being said, it is not as though you will require a full 40 amps at 110 VAC throughout the day. Some loads will only be needed through the night, such as lights. Some loads will only be needed when you engage the load, such as swimming pool pumps. You need to consider your coincidence factor. This relates to how often loads are on. It's perfectly fine to consider your microwave when sizing your solar system, but, realistically, how often is your microwave running? This is a simplified definition of the load factor of a system. This is also why the main incoming circuit breaker from the utility is sized smaller than the addition of all the feeder breakers to household loads. You do not have everything running simultaneously and do not use the amount of electricity that you may believe that you do at any given point in time.

This coincidence factor is defined by how often you have your loads running on an average basis, and you should always cater to a worst-case scenario when you run loads more often than usual. It is basically figuring out how often your loads will run together because loads running together will draw a large amount of power. If you have a 15 A socket and three loads that require 5 A each, how often will you run these three loads together? It's like running your fridge, toaster, and microwave at the same time. This would be a highly unusual scenario, so perhaps you would only ever run two out of these three loads at any given time. What these two fundamentals translate to is that you may have a 15 A socket but will probably only ever have a maximum of 10 A being used 10% of the time, and it may only run 5 A the other 90% of the time. This can help you in specifying your battery storage requirements. In order to calculate your battery size from your current or power requirement, you need to make use of the following equations:

Power (W) = Current (A) x Voltage (V)

Energy (Wh) = Power (W) x Time (Hours)

Battery demand (Ah) = Energy (Wh) / Battery voltage (V)

Battery size (Ah) = Battery Demand (Ah) / Depth of Discharge (%)

Number of batteries = Battery size (Ah) / Single Battery size available (Ah)

Basically, if you wish to power a socket rated for 15 A at a 10 A level for a 12 hour period, then the battery size you require can be calculated in the following way:

Power = current (10 A) x voltage (110 V, the standard voltage in the US)

Power = 10 x 110 = 1,150 W

Energy = 1,150 W x 12 hours = 13,800 Wh

Battery demand (Ah) = Energy (Wh) / AC Voltage (VAC) = 13,800 Wh / 12 V = 1,150 Ah

Now, let's assume that the battery that you wish to select has a depth of discharge of 60%:

Battery size (Ah) = Battery total rating (Ah) / Depth of discharge (%) = 1,150 Ah / 0.6 = 1,917 Ah

Next, you need to take into consideration a battery rating that you may have selected. The battery datasheet will provide you with the Ah rating as well as the depth of discharge. Assume you wish to use 200 Ah batteries and that the 60% depth of discharge used above is in line with the batteries' capability:

Number of batteries = Battery requirement (Ah) / Battery rating (Ah) = 1,1917 Ah / 200 Ah = 9.5 (round up to 10 batteries)

This doesn't consider your coincidence and load factors, which will decrease the number of batteries that you require considerably. Let's say that you wish to have power available for your 15 A socket but will only use a 5 A load for a total of 24 hours to power a fridge. Let's say that you have an additional two 2 A loads that you will only use half of the time. Let's assume one of these is to feed your lights, and the other is to power electronics to charge your phone and other devices. This means that your coincidence factor is 1 for the 5 A fridge load and 0.5 for the 2 A light and charger loads. Now, to determine your coincidence factor, you must consider how often the loads will run simultaneously. As we have mentioned, the fridge will run the entire time, coinciding with both the other loads. However, how often will you run the lights and charging devices together? Most likely, only at night when you require the lights, so you can assume a coincidence factor of 0.75. This means that three-quarters of the time that these devices operate, they will be operating simultaneously. Your overall load demand changes substantially because of this and can be worked out as a percentage of the original 10 A that you had planned for using the following simplified weighted equations:

Load Demand (A) x Load factor (%) x Coincidence Factor (%) = Actual Demand (A)

This can be used to calculate each contributing load and added together to come to a weighted average. In this example, we have three loads to consider as follows:

1. Fridge Load Demand (10 Amps) x Load Factor (1.0) x Coincidence Factor (1.0) = Actual Fridge Demand (5 Amps)

2. Light Load Demand (2 Amps) x Load Factor (0.5) x Coincidence Factor (0.75) = Actual Light Demand (0.75 Amps)

3. Charger Load Demand (2 Amps) x Load Factor (0.5) x Coincidence Factor (0.75) = Actual Charger Demand (0.75 Amps)

Total of the Actual Demand Loads = 5 Amps + 0.75 Amps + 0.75 Amps = 6.5 Amps

This is essentially 65% of the size you had catered for, meaning that the 10 batteries you initially thought you would require could be reduced to eight units, as an even number of batteries is ideal.

This is just a simple rule of thumb method to calculate the basics without considering all the complex factors that can go with it. This rule of thumb calculates how many batteries and panels are required, what your cable size should be, and what inverter rating you need is accurate by over 95%, so it's a good starting point for your system (Energy Matters, n.d.). You may go through a few more iterations of your design after the first one. This is particularly true if the original cost is very high or if the inverters, batteries, and panels on the market don't accurately match your design. You may also find that you hadn't considered a factor, such as the DC voltage of your strings, and that changes your entire design.

One of the most important aspects to consider with your solar system is weight. This is especially true for a system mounted on the roof of a house or a structure, such as an RV. Most vehicles will be constructed with a chassis or body that can support additional weight but may completely alter gravity. With any moving body, the center of gravity completely alters the handling of a vehicle. Turning will be more sluggish, and the risk of rolling or suffering from understeer is a major concern. Understeer is when you turn the vehicle, but it feels as though it has a delay and pulls you toward the straight line of your trajectory for your approach to a turn.

For non-mobile installations, the primary concern is the structural integrity of the installation. If you have a rooftop that was constructed to hold roof tiles only, and you feel as though you cannot walk on the roof to inspect it because it is creaking under your weight, then the chances of that same roof being able to support several solar panels are next to nothing. Each individual solar panel that is 2 m by 1 m, or 3 ft by 6 ft, weighs roughly 20 kilograms, or 45 pounds, excluding the mounting structure and equipment required for it. This is not considering the additional force experienced from wind, rain, hail, snow, or any other weather condition.

You must be aware of the structure you will mount your solar panels on, where the points of reinforcement are, and how it may affect your property or vehicle insurance. Again, it is essential to highlight the kill switch and minuscule increase in fire risk of a solar system in any installation to keep a low insurance premium on your asset. When sizing your load requirements, it is best to look at your structure and determine the weight capacity of the existing structure. It isn't much of a concern for RVs or boats, as they can handle the additional weight on top of the main chassis. When it comes to cabins and tiny houses, the roofs may not be able to handle an additional 300 kgs or 700 pounds. Be cautious in these scenarios, as a roof may be able to take this additional weight as a static object, but that does not mean that it can handle this additional weight in a thunderstorm or if there is a significant amount of wind or snow. It may also result in an insurance nightmare where a roof was designed on standard applications of handling weather effects, and now you are adding another component to this. It's always a good idea to look at the building blueprints to see the size and weight capacity of the roof before installing your solar system. It's also valuable in this instance to enquire what the implications would be. It's not worth it to add your solar system only for a terrible occurrence, such as a natural disaster, to happen, and insurance companies refuse to cover the damage because of the addition of a solar system.

When sizing the required load of your system, particularly a house system, the best way to determine an accurate requirement is to look at your existing utility bill. The monthly bill that you are provided based on your energy meter readings is typically determined in kWh. With this reference, you should be able to average out your annual requirements for any home or holiday home application. If you are using an average of 10 kWh per day, you will be able to size your entire system based on this, including losses due to efficiency. All solar systems experience inefficiency, and you have to cater to unexpected weather conditions which may hinder your system's ability to generate power due to overcast weather or an unusually long period where your energy demands are far higher than usual.

To do this, take your monthly average utility bill over 12 months. Then take this value and divide it by an average of 30 days to get your daily energy usage. Let's say that this value comes to 5 units, or kWh, per day for a small home. This amounts to average daily usage. In order to determine your inverter size, number and size of solar panels, and number and size of batteries, you should use similar calculations used above. The primary difference is that all power used needs to be generated by the solar panels themselves. So, take your 5 kWh per day, cater to your efficiency losses, and allow a 25% safety factor.

A safety factor is an engineering term used in situations where you need to overcompensate because too many variables are unaccounted for and cannot be accurately calculated or predicted. The weather falls under this category, which is why your safety factor is required to be so substantial. Considering this, you need to allow for flexibility to cater for 7.5 kWh per day on average. Including efficiency from your DC system to your AC system requires you to implement the following calculation:

Solar Power requirement (DC kWh) = Power Demand (AC kWh) / Predicted overall efficiency (%)

Power Requirement = 7.5 kWh / 0.85 = 8.83 kWh per day. Average this up to 9 kWhdc per day.

This amount of power per day requires that you have solar panels that can provide this power in just the number of PSH per day. So, if you require 9 kWh in the space of 24 hours, then your solar panels need to generate at least this amount while the sun is up. Let's use the annual average for the sun being out and calculate PSH to be 7 hours per day. This necessitates that the DC system and solar system demand is as follows:

Solar DC demand (kW) = Calculated Demand (kWhdc) / Peak Sun Hours (Hours)

Solar demand (kW) = 9 / 7 = 1.28 kW

Now take this value and consider that days of overcast weather or reduced sun content result in a lack of generation ability from your solar panels. This can be averaged over the space of a year when considering the number of days of sun and the number of days of overcast weather. Let's assume a situation where the sun is only expected to shine for half of the year. This equates to a safety factor of two in order to ensure that you can generate enough power in a single sunny day to last over two days without any other form of power generation.

Solar Supply (kW) = Solar demand (kW) x (Days of sunlight per year / Total days per year)

Solar supply = 1.28kW x (182.5/365) = 2.6 kW

Now, this is starting to line up to a solar array size in a more understandable manner. It would be best to look at the solar panel sizes available on the market for your usage and allow yourself to generate enough power for your current system while allowing for future expansion. It is advisable to size your solar panels to cater to this demand with one additional panel and size your battery system and inverter for 1.5 times.

If you use 360 W solar panels, as 360 W and 320 W solar panels are most readily available, then you will require:

Number of panels = Power demand (kW) / Solar panel size (kW)

Number of panels = 2.6 / 0.4 = 6.5 panels

For this requirement, seven solar panels sized at 400 W or eight panels rated at 360 W should be enough for this system. Determining the number of panels that you require is the first step to take.

The next thing that you should determine is how you will hook up your solar panels. Let's take the typical example covered above, where a 360W solar panel is selected. Will you connect these eight panels in series to form a single string, which is possible to do? To calculate if this is possible, you need to find the voltage of the solar panels by referring to their datasheet. Most datasheets will list the operational voltage as Vmax or Vmp. This is the maximum operating voltage of each solar system, assuming ideal conditions of high solar irradiance and a temperature lower than 25 degrees Celsius, or 77 degrees Fahrenheit. This is not to be mistaken with Voc, which is also typically listed on solar panel datasheets. These values are when the solar panels are open-circuited or not connected to an inverter, with no current flowing through them.

When you connect solar panels in series, you add their voltage in order to get the total voltage. It is the same concept as connecting batteries together in series, with each battery adding to the overall system voltage across all the batteries. Let's use a typical voltage rating for a single 360 W CanadianSolar solar panel at 45 Volts to continue the example used above. To calculate your entire string voltage, use the following equation:

String Voltage (VDC) = Individual Panel Voltage (VDC) x Number of Panels (per unit)

String Voltage (VDC) = 45 VDC x 8 panels = 360 VDC

Now that you have the string voltage, you can specify an inverter based on the power output requirements and input voltage requirements. Most single-phase inverters rated for approximately 5 kW will handle 360 VDC as the solar array input voltage.

It's always good practice to slightly oversize your solar inverter to cater to expanding your solar array size. If you mount these eight panels now, but you realize that you require more power in five years, you want to add more panels rather than have to replace your inverter for a larger unit completely.

One of the biggest disadvantages of going with a built-in charge controller unit versus a separate unit is that, if the unit fails or you are having trouble with it, you will need to replace your entire inverter, or at the very least have the entire system offline until maintenance or repair work is carried out. Compare this to a separate charge controller, which could be disconnected and replaced at a much lower cost. Many charge controllers are manufactured to work alongside a specific solar inverter, so be sure to pay attention to which units are compatible with one another. An excellent strategy to follow is to stick to the same brand to ensure that connectivity and interconnection of control and monitoring are compatible. If you decide to use a Sunny Boy inverter, try to combine it with a Sunny Boy battery charger. Likewise, if you select a Victron solar inverter, a solar charge controller and MPPT module will work best in conjunction with this product. This is also true for warranty purposes. One manufacturer providing all the devices will make it more straightforward to identify problems, rectify them, and have replacement components sent from the manufacturer without warranty claim issues.

CONCLUSION

The information that you have gathered throughout this book should enable you to go out there and purchase and install your first solar system. It may have seemed daunting at first, but it is very doable when you break down the overall design into smaller, more manageable tasks. It would be best to look at what you want to get out of the solar system and determine the specific area to install the solar system. It may be on an RV, a tiny house, a boat, or even a trailer. There are so many applications for solar systems, and being able to generate your own electricity, even in remote areas, without having to burn fuel, such as with a generator, is such a valuable asset to have.

Once you have determined your specific application, you need to know some of the general terms of electricity, specifically related to solar panels. You need to have a basic understanding of your voltage, current, and power, as well as the differences between AC and DC power. Another valuable bit of knowledge is in the components themselves, including protection, earthing, inverters, and cables. There is no point in going ahead and installing your own solar system if you have no idea what the different components do and the basics of how they work. The better you understand your system, the more empowered you will be to maintain or repair the system if it stops functioning the way it is supposed to. It's also crucial to have this knowledge so that you can remain safe from harm, especially from electrocution. Suppose you want to follow quality and safety standards, especially when you install, test, or do maintenance on your solar system. In that case, you should have a solar system that meets all international standards.

When selecting your batteries, it is crucial to know the difference between the various batteries on the market. You won't want to purchase liquid lead acid batteries if an AGM battery works far better for your particular requirements. You also need to know what to look out for in batteries, including their voltage, amp hour rating, physical size, depth of discharge, and all the other pros and cons associated with each battery. When confronted with several options, you need to look at what will work best for you and offer you backup power when you need it rather than run out of energy in the middle of the night, leaving you in a blackout situation. Make sure you store your batteries in a suitable location, carry out maintenance if and when necessary, connect your batteries correctly to the charge controller, inverter, or battery charger, and don't overwork your batteries and end up reducing their life span by several years. You also need to be fully conscious of your budget and how much you are willing to spend, as well as how often you will make use of your batteries. If you spend more on a high-end battery, it will last you far longer and, possibly, save you more money in the long run.

Once you have selected a suitable battery type, you need to look at the solar panels you wish to invest in. These components, along with the inverter, will be the three most significant expenses of any solar system. Choosing the right type of solar panel for yourself is also based on your application and what you hope to get out of the system. Flexible solar panels may be more suitable for vehicles, such as RV's and boats, whereas rigid panels may be more suitable for houses. You may also want to consider monocrystalline panels if you don't have a lot of physical space but want to maximize the solar system's energy output. If this isn't as important as the cost for you, then a polycrystalline panel option may be best suited to fit your needs. Keep an eye out for panels built to international standards of safety and quality, and try to choose panels with a higher energy output to get the most power out of the fewest number of panels.

You also need to decide how you want to connect your panels. There is a limit to the number of panels that you can connect in series, and the solar inverter that you connect will also have a restriction on the number of strings and combined voltage of a string, so be sure not to exceed these limitations. It's always an option to purchase a few panels to install now and expand your system at a later stage. It's also important to note that you don't necessarily need to have a large number of panels if you have a backup battery system. If you can keep the batteries fully charged when the sun is out throughout the day, why add more panels only to waste the excess power?

Now that you have your batteries and solar panels selected, you need to look at the type and size of the inverter that you need. You may require having more than one MPPT on your inverter to capture the early morning and late afternoon sun more effectively. This is a great feature, as it allows you to connect two or more strings to separate inputs and maximizes your power generation capabilities throughout the day. It's an ideal way to do this without the expense of a tracking system, where the solar panels track the sun in the sky throughout the day. Another important consideration when selecting your inverter is confirming the efficiency, installation requirements, environmental rating (especially the operational temperature range), and power rating. You have to ensure that the inverter you select is large enough to handle the amount of power generated from your solar panels and convert that DC power to more usable AC power without significant losses.

When specifying inverters, a final note is that you should save in cost and space if you find a product that already has a built-in charge controller and connection for batteries. In this way, you will have a central unit that handles your solar panels, battery charging, and discharging and supplies AC power per your demand. Several major manufacturers produce inverters like this. Although they may be more expensive, they are worth investing in, as they are typically cheaper than purchasing both an inverter and a charge controller.

Now that you have all the major components for your solar system, you need to ensure that you have all the correct tools and equipment to mount your solar panels in your designated area safely. Do not forget that solar panels generate a voltage as soon as they are exposed to sunlight, so care must be taken when connecting the solar panels in a string and to the inverter. Electrocution from the panels themselves may not be lethal, but there are major risks, given you may be working at height and could potentially fall after being shocked.

Most tools that are required are typical electrician tools. You need a crimping tool, multimeter, screwdrivers, spanners, Allen wrenches, wire strippers, and a clamp meter for all installation and functional test work. Sometimes, if you are building a frame or mounting solar panels to an RV or boat roof, you will require some power tools, including a drill and angle grinder. It is advisable to use battery-operated power tools to have them handy in any location.

Take care to follow all manufacturer specifications when carrying out the installation. If the inverter installation guide informs you that the inverter must be installed in an upright position, then you must follow this guideline. This is especially relevant when it comes to battery storage. Great care must be taken to store batteries safely.

You now have all the basic knowledge to put together your very own solar system! As you can now see, it isn't overly complicated to follow the basic steps in specifying the major components that are best suited to your needs. You also understand the basic practices for installing your solar system safely and sticking to quality and safety standards in your installation. You now are also more knowledgeable than the average person and will be able to tell if a salesperson is pushing his product on you or is trying to find the right product for your requirements, which enables you to avoid buying unnecessary components and missing out on buying parts with significant value to you.

Building your own solar setup is very rewarding and will allow you to save on electricity costs in the long run. It will enable you to use your own power and know exactly where that power came from. Whether your system is mobile or non-mobile, you will be able to generate electricity to use from the sun, will not be impacted by problems on the grid, such as blackout scenarios, and will benefit on a monetary level in the long run. This is an investment and should be viewed as the valuable asset that it is. This is also a way for you to reduce your carbon footprint and ensure that the power you use has been generated from a renewable source. We at Small Footprint Press recognize the importance of reducing our carbon footprint to live more sustainably in the twenty-first century. Every bit counts and every individual who takes the initiative to be more conscious of their impact on the environment has the ability to make a difference. If we all make these changes in our lifestyle, we will continue to thrive and avoid damaging the environment globally. You can make a difference, and if everyone realized that their efforts and contributions made an impact, then millions more would be more proactive in reducing their carbon footprint.

You can now go out and start creating your own system. There is nothing to lose in designing and pricing your system and working out the buy-back period of the system to start you off. There is no rush, and it is better to be thorough and do things right the first time than having to make changes later, which could be time-consuming or expensive. Get your design ready, then check on the various products available to you on the market today. Look out for specials and deals to maximize your cost-saving. Once you have installed your system and have it up and running, you will wonder how you ever operated without it before!

REFERENCES

Average Annual Precipitation for Missouri. (n.d.). Current Results. https://www.currentresults.com/Weather/Missouri/average-yearly-precipitation.php

Buri, R. (2017). Solar-roof-solar-energy. In *pixabay.com.* https://cdn.pixabay.com/photo/2017/08/21/20/29/solar-2666770_960_720.jpg

Cloud, B. (2018). Lake in forest. In *unsplash.com.* https://images.unsplash.com/photo-1542849922-a7e0aeb0ff84?ixlib=rb-1.2.1&ixid=MnwxMjA3fDB8MHxwaG90by1wYWdlfHx8fGVufDB8fHx8&auto=format&fit=crop&w=1534&q=80

Dais, W. (2011). chicken-coop-farm-chickens-coop. In *pixabay.com.* https://cdn.pixabay.com/photo/2014/05/14/08/02/chicken-coop-343942_960_720.jpg

Ellis, K. (2018). Triangle house. In *unsplash.com.* https://images.unsplash.com/photo-1525113990976-399835c43838?ixid=MnwxMjA3fDB8MHxwaG90by1wYWdlfHx8fGVufDB8fHx8&ixlib=rb-1.2.1&auto=format&fit=crop&w=700&q=80

Giannatti, D. (2019). Outhouse door. In *unsplash.com.* https://images.unsplash.com/photo-1548097751-193b78ef6823?ixid=MnwxMjA3fDB8MHxwaG90by1wYWdlfHx8fGVufDB8fHx8&ixlib=rb-1.2.1&auto=format&fit=crop&w=639&q=80

Glenn, K. (2018). Green dome near brown wooden dock. In *unsplash.com.* https://images.unsplash.com/photo-1521401830884-6c03c1c87ebb?ixlib=rb-1.2.1&ixid=MnwxMjA3fDB8MHxwaG90by1wYWdlfHx8fGVufDB8fHx8&auto=format&fit=crop&w=1500&q=80

Gomez, J. (2019). Wood stove. In *unsplash.com.* https://images.unsplash.com/photo-1564848534637-f57f9b1eb36e?ixlib=rb-1.2.1&ixid=MnwxMjA3fDB8MHxwaG90by1wYWdlfHx8fGVufDB8fHx8&auto=format&fit=crop&w=632&q=80

Gruebner, O., Rapp, M. A., Adli, M., Kluge, U., Galea, S., & Heinz, A. (2017). Cities and Mental Health. *Deutsches Arzteblatt international, 114*(8), 121–127. https://doi.org/10.3238/arztebl.2017.0121

How We Use Water. (n.d.). United States Environmental Protection Agency (EPA). https://www.epa.gov/watersense/how-we-use-water

Jesus, J. (n.d.). Photo-of-man-standing-surrounded-by-green-leaf-plants. In *pexels.com.* https://images.pexels.com/photos/1084540/pexels-photo-1084540.jpeg?auto=compress&cs=tinysrgb&dpr=2&h=650&w=940

Lechner, G. (2020). Black and white wooden house. In *unsplash.com.* https://images.unsplash.com/photo-1580856942656-d4416b6e5c2e?ixlib=rb-1.2.1&ixid=MnwxMjA3fDB8MHxwaG90by1wYWdlfHx8fGVufDB8fHx8&auto=format&fit=crop&w=1563&q=80

Living, O. G. (2020, February 26). *How to go off grid for $10k or less*. Off Grid Living. https://offgridliving.net/go-off-grid-10k/

PublicDomainPictures. (2010). Clean-countryside-drink-garden. In *pixabay.com*. https://cdn.pixabay.com/photo/2012/03/03/22/59/clean-21479_960_720.jpg

Timmer, K. (2019). Brown wood house. In *unsplash.com*. https://images.unsplash.com/photo-1568659585069-facb248c4935?ixlib=rb-1.2.1&ixid=MnwxMjA3fDB8MHxwaG90by1wYWdlfHx8fGVufDB8fHx8&auto=format&fit=crop&w=1500&q=80

Almerini, A. (2021, March 5). *Everything you need to know about installing solar panels on boats*. Solar reviews. https://www.solarreviews.com/blog/solar-panels-for-boats

Crown Battery. (2018, April 24). *What is a deep cycle battery?* https://www.crownbattery.com/news/what-is-a-deep-cycle-battery-

Clifton, S. (2016, October 5). *How to fuse your solar system*. Renogy United States. https://www.renogy.com/blog/how-to-fuse-your-solar-system/

De Rooij, D. (2020, July 27). *Solar panel angle: How to calculate solar panel tilt angle?* Sinovoltaics - Zero risk SolarTM. https://sinovoltaics.com/learning-center/system-design/solar-panel-angle-tilt-calculation/

Dennis, R. (2019, December 20). *How to install a solar panel system on your RV roof*. RV mods - RV guides - RV tips | DoItYourselfRV. https://www.doityourselfrv.com/solar-power-4/

Energy Matters. (n.d.). *Deep cycle battery guide*. https://www.energymatters.com.au/components/batteries/#battery-explanation

Enphase. (n.d.). *What is the difference between a watt and a watt-hour?* https://enphase.com/en-us/support/what-difference-between-watt-and-watt-hour

Going Solar. (2019, March 28). *How are solar panels attached to your roof? Solar panel installation*. https://goingsolar.com/how-are-solar-panels-attached-to-your-roof-solar-panel-installation/

GridFree. (2019, August 12). *Off-grid basics - Solar power systems 102*. https://gridfree.store/blogs/how-to-articles/off-grid-basics-solar-power-systems-101

Hutchison, D., & Galiardi, S. (2019, February 21). *How solar panels work: breaking it down for beginners*. Renogy United States. https://www.renogy.com/blog/how-solar-panels-work-breaking-it-down-for-beginners/

Marsh, J. (2019, January 19). *What is solar energy?* EnergySage. https://news.energysage.com/what-is-solar-energy/

Matasci, S. (2019, January 29). *Ground mount solar panels: Top 3 things you need to know*. EnergySage. https://news.energysage.com/ground-mounted-solar-panels-top-3-things-you-need-to-know/

Proinso. (2020, May 23). *8 steps to building a DIY off-grid solar system*. https://www.proinso.net/blogs/build-diy-off-grid-solar-system/

Prowse Publications LLC. (n.d. a). *Large RV solar power blueprints.* Mobile solar power made easy. https://www.mobile-solarpower.com/the-off-grid-king-power-anything.html

Prowse Publications LLC. (n.d. b). *RV solar power blueprints.* Mobile solar power made easy. https://www.mobile-solarpower.com/the-classic-400-watt-rvs-vans-buses.html

Prowse Publications LLC. (n.d. c). *Tools.* Mobile solar power made easy. https://www.mobile-solarpower.com/tools.html

Prowse Publications LLC. (n.d. d). *Van Dweller solar power blueprints.* Mobile solar power made easy. https://www.mobile-solarpower.com/the-minimalist-great-for-small-vans-and-cars.html

ShopSolarKits.com. (n.d.). *Solar load calculator | How much solar do I need?* https://shopsolarkits.com/pages/watt-hour-calculator

Solar 4 RVs. (n.d.). *What's watt? How to calculate watt hours.* https://www.solar4rvs.com.au/buying/buyer-guides/assessing-your-solar-needs/calculating-watt-hours-wh-kwh/

Svarc, J. (2019, December 19). *Top 7 solar myths busted.* Clean energy reviews. https://www.cleanenergyreviews.info/blog/top-myths-about-solar-panels

Talens Peiró, L., Villalba Méndez, G., & Ayres, R. U. (2013). *Lithium: Sources, production, uses, and recovery outlook.* JOM, 65(8), 986–996. https://doi.org/10.1007/s11837-013-0666-4

Unbound Solar. (2020, July 8). *Grid-tied vs. off-grid solar: which is right for you?* https://unboundsolar.com/blog/grid-tied-vs-off-grid-solar

Wallender, L. (2020, July 10). *The difference between watts vs. volts.* The Spruce. https://www.thespruce.com/the-difference-between-watts-vs-volts-4767057

Weir, M. (2018, July 18). *The complete guide to solar panel mounts for boats (and where to position them)* BetterBoat. https://betterboat.com/boating/solar-panel-mounts-for-boats/